A CHANGED LIFE

This book is dedicated to-

God's New Life Mission

**without whose help this work
could not have been completed.
They do a miraculous service for
people in need and operate as God's
helpers here on Earth.**

**"I've never met an addict that lived happily
ever after and I have known many.
Jail, prison and death is how that life ends."**
Quote from a participant in 'God's New Life'

A CHANGED LIFE

Introduction

I suppose there is a time in everyone's life when they must decide whether to stay in the sad state they are in or whether to reach down into the core of their very being and make a definitive, permanent change for the better. When a person gets to that point they are usually ready to accept any way out and willing to do whatever it takes to get to their goal of a better life.

Whether it is for the sake of just themselves or themselves plus their loved ones, they are willing to put that one foot forward and step out in faith alone in the hope that their goal will be accomplished.   What do you have to lose when you have lost it all already?

The stories in this book are just those kind- people who have taken that leap of faith.   There has been no other way out, tried everything, lost it all, nothing has worked, sank deeper into the miry pit with only a pinkie finger left grasping for the light.

In that one last desperate moment of life, that bottom of the pit, you can either decide to give up, find the peace of death and let that pinkie finger slide on under.....or you discover there is deep within you a hidden away cleft, a barely visible spark that still clings to life, a hope, a desire, a sheer will to survive, a refusal to go under.   A voice cries out within "Somebody help me!"

Guess who is waiting to hear that cry?   He has been yearning, begging, pleading, protecting you from certain death at times, keeping a watchful eye out for you, waiting for you to call.

He instantly reaches down and grabs hold of that pinkie finger and plucks you up out of the pit, then sets your feet on firm ground, cleans you up, refreshes you, nourishes you and gives you that abundant life you have longed for.   He IS that spark within you, He IS that life you desire, He IS that hope for a better life!   HE is God.

These are the stories of those who have reached that point of decision--either I keep going like I am and die in this miserable state or I make this one last ditch effort to live a better life.   They have been to the extreme bad and made their way back to a life of meaning with goals to achieve, a hope-filled and brighter place than they were in.

These people deserve much praise for making that decision.   Not all people in the pit make it out.   Some sadly choose to let that pinkie go under, never to see the light again.   It takes great courage and faith to step out and decide you want a complete change, to turn your life around.

Sometimes they have no means, no money, no home, only the clothes on their backs and even those are ragged.   But they choose to reach out for help one last time and they choose the only ultimate helper, the only one to dry their tears, the only one to meet their needs, the only one who will never forsake them, the only one to make good things happen.   And that one is our Christ, our Savior, our Redeemer, our EVERYTHING!

I have endeavored to write this book because of the epidemic of drug addiction in not only this country but seemingly every country on this planet.   A chain of events down through the ages has given Satan the opportunity to utilize an old play toy of his-drugs.   This toy has always been around and played with over the centuries.   But in the chaotic, wicked, anything goes social climate in this new century, Satan has dragged his old toy out of the closet, shined it up, made it really attractive and fun to play with, given it all sorts of new names, mass produced it, and it is now easily available for sale to the public.   Yes, there is always a price to pay isn't there?

There are various explanations given for becoming addicted to drugs.   I mix alcohol into that category because it is a drug.   People suffering from anxiety, bipolar disorder, depression or other mental illnesses use drugs and alcohol to "level out" their emotional state. They see family members, friends, role models or entertainers using drugs and rationalize that they can too.   Perhaps they become bored and think drugs will help.   They hope drugs will help relieve stress. People figure if a drug is prescribed by a doctor-and those prescriptions are far too easy to obtain now-it must be okay. Many get physically injured and unintentionally get hooked on prescribed drugs. People use drugs to cover painful memories in their past. Some think drugs will help them fit in.   "Chasing that goat" is another reason, meaning to continually chase the high they once experienced.

They will go through drug treatment programs, one after another, be given all kinds of legal drugs to wean them off of the illegal drug their addicted to (why is that okay? I mean, really?). They will go through therapy, psychoanalysis, in-patient treatments, out-patient treatments, be run through the mill and out the door only to relapse very soon after being out.   Why? Because these state/government sponsored (they depend on government/state funds to run their operations and therefore must adhere to governmental regulations) programs have very little concern for their patients anymore.   It has become an insurance rip-off.   You will either need to have insurance that covers the cost or big cash up front if you want help.   When your cash or insurance runs the limit, then you are kicked out onto the street again. "Good luck, we have done all we can do for you--Just say no! Ba-bye." The privately run programs are no better. Most of those are too expensive for the average person. They are definitely out to make a profit in order to keep up and running. So you will pay dearly and when you decide you have had enough, you can simply check yourself out.

I am being somewhat cynical as these places all have different rules and regulations and they do somehow manage to help some people but many are lacking a fundamental premise. For one, taking responsibility for your own actions, your choices, and to stop blaming others for what you have done. They will usually tell you that you have a "disorder" that has caused you to resort to drugs.

However, when you realize that it was you and you alone who made that bad choice, you will slowly come to see yourself for what you are and the brevity of your situation. When your brain is clear, and your eyes are open, then your heart is ready for the krazy glue.....What? Krazy glue? Yes, let me explain. Faith-based programs are statistically very successful in their treatment of drug addiction. Why is that? Because you come to realize that you answer not to the people running the facility or even to yourself but to a much higher power-that of God. When your body rids itself of the toxins that you have ingested and you start really seeing yourself for what you became and who you are and who you now want to be, then you are ready for the potter.   The potter is God Almighty who can take the vessel broken into the tiniest shards, seemingly unfixable and ready for the refuse pile and by His grace and power can grab that wonder working krazy glue of His, namely the blood of His Son, Christ Jesus, and glue you back together, piece by tiny piece, until you are once again whole, gleaming with the brightness of His love!   Amazing isn't it?   Naysayer's will always be around to contest the existence of God.   But just because they say it, that doesn't make it so. God is definitely here.   There is that power that can change lives dramatically and instantly. And when a person gets a good "dose" of God, others will know it. The person is totally different.   They will not walk the old way, talk the old way, live the old way.   A new creature in Christ our Savior will immerge.   He is a life changer.

Thanks to the aid of Gary Still, Assistant Executive Director, and the participants at God's New Life Mission in Marked Tree, Arkansas, I hope to allow you, the reader, to transport yourself into the world of those willing to let you into their most personal stories.   They are as real as it gets.   I have corrected only a small number of spelling/grammatical errors or altered the structure of a sentence here and there for clarification purposes or to keep family members/friends names private. The life stories are one-hundred percent their's.   I am very grateful to them for their honesty and courage in allowing me to lay bare the mistakes in life they have made so that others might not follow their path.

There are seven stories in this book of people who have lived through the hellish nightmares of drug addiction.   What it can lead you into, where it will take you, what it will make you do, where it will dump you when it has wasted you away. The stories were signed by the participants when I received them but I have chosen to make them somewhat anonymous, only their initials will be used.   Not only to protect their identities but because these are stories, while unique to the person who wrote them, are identical to situations that are happening right now to millions of individuals in the world who are tortured by addiction.   I decided to progress by their dates of birth. Only their age and whether male or female will be revealed.   My intent is to show what led them down the path they chose and how they have pulled themselves out of it by the help of God and Him leading them in the direction of people who can help them.

I have been guilty of thinking that I would never do the kinds of things that are portrayed in these stories.   I was raised in a good home with parents who loved me and taught me right from wrong.   But several of these stories are from homes just like I had.   So social status, bank accounts, church membership, age--none of these make a person exempt from the black pit that is drug addiction.   We should not judge them for their misdeeds because "but for the grace of God, there go I".

I have begun with a bit of background history of drug use since record keeping in this world began teamed with the cumulative knowledge of archaeological evidence that has been uncovered.   As is plain throughout history, drug use has traveled through time right alongside of mankind, in every tribe, nation, race, and continent on the face of this earth.   All the drugs known now to mankind are made with substances available on this planet.   However, though God made all these ingredients, He is by no means faulty because He created them.   He created all things on this planet for the good of mankind.   It is what *man's* accumulated knowledge does with these components that makes the difference, whether we use the substances for good or abuse them.

Please read these true stories of hopelessness and redemption.   I trust they will stir your heart as they did mine. These souls are the embodiment of who Christ came to save and what He wants to do for all of mankind.

THE HISTORY OF DRUGS

SOURCE:
WWW.INPUD.WORDPRESS.COM

SUMMARY OF HISTORICAL EVENTS IN THE
HISTORY OF DRUGS

Source: www.inpud.wordpress.com

B.C.

5000 B.C. The Sumerians use opium, suggested by the fact that they have an ideogram for it which has been translated as HUL, meaning "joy" or "rejoicing." [Alfred R. Lindensmith, *Addiction and Opiates.* p. 207]

3500 B.C. Earliest historical record of the production of alcohol: the description of a brewery in an Egyptian papyrus. [Joel Fort, *The Pleasure Seekers*, p. 14]

3000 B.C. Approximate date of the supposed origin of the use of tea in China.

2500 B.C. Earliest historical evidence of the eating of poppy seeds among the Lake Dwellers on Switzerland. [Ashley Montagu, The long search for euphoria, *Reflections*, 1:62-69 (May-June), 1966; p. 66]

2000 B.C. Earliest record of prohibitionist teaching, by an Egyptian priest, who writes to his pupil: "I, thy superior, forbid thee to go to the taverns. Thou art degraded like beasts." [W.F. Crafts *et al*., *Intoxicating Drinks and Drugs*, p. 5]

350 B.C. Proverbs, 31:6-7: "Give strong drink to him who is ready to perish, and wine unto those that be of heavy hearts.   Let him drink, and forget his poverty, and remember his misery no more." (KJV Bible)

300 B.C. Theophrastus (371-287 B.C.), Greek naturalist and philosopher, records what has remained as the earliest undisputed reference to the use of poppy juice.

250 B.C. Psalms, 104:14-15: "He causeth the grass to grow for the cattle, and herb for the service of man: that he may bring forth food out of the earth; and wine that maketh glad the heart of man....." (KJV Bible)

A.D.
350 A.D. Earliest mention of tea, in a Chinese dictionary.

4th century St. John Chrysostom (345-407), Bishop of Constantinople: "I hear man cry, 'Would there be no wine! O folly! O madness!' Is it wine that causes this abuse? No, for if you say, 'Would there were no light!' because of the informers, and would there were no women because of adultery." [Quoted in Berton Roueche, *The Neutral Spirit*, pp. 150-151]

450 Babylonian Talmud: "Wine is at the head of all medicines; where wine is lacking, drugs are necessary." [Quoted in Burton Stevenson (Ed.), *The Macmillan Book of Proverbs*, p. 21]
c. 1000 Opium is widely used in China and the far East. [Alfred A. Lindensmith, *The Addict and the Law*, p. 194]

Tobacco smoking is introduced to Europe by Columbus in 1493 from America.

c. 1500 According to J.D. Rolleston, a British medical historian, a medieval Russian cure for drunkenness consisted in "taking a piece of pork, putting it secretly in a Jew's bed for nine days, and then giving it to the drunkard in a pulverized form, who will turn away from drinking as a Jew would from pork." [Quoted in Roueche, op. cit. p. 144]

c. 1525 Paracelsus (1490-1541) introduces laudanum, or tincture of opium, into the practice of medicine.

1600 Shakespeare: "Falstaff. . . . If I had a thousand sons the first human principle I would teach them should be, to foreswear thin portions and to addict themselves to sack." ("Sack" is an obsolete term for "sweet wine" like sherry). [William Shakespeare, *Second Part of King Henry the Fourth*, Act IV, Scene III, lines 133-136]

17th century   The prince of the petty state of Waldeck pays ten halers to anyone who denounces a coffee drinker. [Griffith Edwards, Psychoactive substances, *The Listener*, March 23, 1972, pp. 360-363; p.361]

17th century   In Russia, Czar Michael Federovitch executes anyone on whom tobacco is found. "Czar Alexei Mikhailovitch rules that anyone caught with tobacco should be tortured until he gave up the name of the supplier." [Ibid.]

1613   John Rolf, the husband of the Indian princess Pocahontas, sends the first shipment of Virginia tobacco from Jamestown to England.

c. 1650   The use of tobacco is prohibited in Bavaria, Saxony, and in Zurich, but the prohibitions are ineffective. Sultan Murad IV of the Ottoman Empire decrees the death penalty for smoking tobacco: "Wherever there Sultan went on his travels or on a military expedition his halting-places were always distinguished by a terrible rise in executions. Even on the battlefield he was fond of surprising men in the act of smoking, when he would punish them by beheading, hanging, quartering or crushing their hands and feed. . . . Nevertheless, in spite of all the horrors and persecution. . . the passion for smoking still persisted." [Edward M. Brecher et al., *Licit and Illicit Drugs*, p. 212]

1680   Thomas Syndenham (1625-80): "Among the remedies which it has pleased the Almighty God to give to man to relieve his sufferings, none is so universal and efficacious as opium." [Quoted in Louis Goodman and Alfred Gilman, *The Pharmacological Basis of Therapeutics*, First Edition (1941), p. 186]

1690   The "Act for the Encouraging of the Distillation of Brandy and Spirits from Corn" is enacted in England. [Roueche, op. cit. p. 27]

1691   In Lundeberg, Germany, the penalty for smoking (tobacco) is death.

1717   Liquor licenses in Middlesex (England) are granted only to those who "would take oaths of allegiance and of belief in the King's supremacy over the Church" [G.E.G. Catlin, *Liquor Control*, p. 14]

1736   The Gin Act (England) is enacted with the avowed object of making spirits "come so dear to the consumer that the poor will not be able to launch into excessive use of them." This effort results in general lawbreaking and fails to halt the steady rise in the consumption of even legally produced and sold liquor. [Ibid., p. 15]

1745   The magistrates of one London division demanded that "publicans and wine-merchants should swear that they anathematized the doctrine of Transubstantiation." [Ibid., p. 14]

Dover's Powders, opium preparation used for 150 years, 1762 Thomas Dover, and English physician, introduces his prescription for a diaphoretic powder, which he recommends mainly for the treatment of gout. Soon named "Dover's Powder," this compound becomes the most widely used opium preparation during the next 150 years.

1785   Benjamin Rush publishes his *Inquiry into the Effects of Ardent Spirits on the Human Body and Mind*; in it, he calls the intemperate use of distilled spirits a "disease," and estimates the annual rate of death due to alcoholism in the United States as "not less than 4,000 people" in a population then of less than 6 million. [Quoted in S. S. Rosenberg (Ed.), *Alcohol and Health*, p. 26]

1789   The first American temperance society is formed in Litchfield, Connecticut. [Crafts et. al., op. cit., p. 9]

1790   Benjamin Rush persuades his associates at the Philadelphia College of Physicians to send an appeal to Congress to "impose such heavy duties upon all distilled spirits as shall be effective to restrain their intemperate use in the country." [Quoted in ibid.]

1792   The first prohibitory laws against opium in China are promulgated. The punishment decreed for keepers of opium shops is strangulation.

1792   The Whisky Rebellion, a protest by farmers in western Pennsylvania against a federal tax on liquor, breaks out and is put down by overwhelming force sent to the area by George Washington.   Samuel Taylor Coleridge writes "Kublai Khan" while under the influence of opium.

1800   Napoleon's army, returning from Egypt, introduces cannabis (hashish, marijuana) into France. Avant-garde artists and writers in Paris develop their own cannabis ritual, leading, in 1844, to the establishment of *Le Club de Haschischins.* [William A. Emboden, Jr., Ritual Use of Cannabis Sativa L.: A historical-ethnographic survey, in Peter T. Furst (Ed.), *Flesh of the Gods*, pp. 214-236; pp. 227-228]

1801   On Jefferson's recommendation, the federal duty

tax on liquor was abolished. [Catlin, op. cit., p. 113]

1804   Thomas Trotter, an Edinburgh physician, publishes *An Essay, Medical, Philosophical, and Chemical on Drunkenness and Its Effects on the Human Body*: "In medical language, I consider drunkenness, strictly speaking, to be a disease, produced by a remote cause, and giving birth to actions and movements in the living body that disorder the functions of health. . . The habit of drunkenness is a disease of the mind." [Quoted in Roueche, op. cit. pp. 87-88]

1805   Friedrich Wilhelm Adam Serturner, a German chemist, isolates and describes morphine.

Confessions of an English Opium Eater, 1822

1822   Thomas De Quincey's *Confessions of an English Opium Eater* is published. He notes that the opium habit, like any other habit, must be learned: "Making allowance for constitutional differences, I should say that *in less than 120 days* no habit of opium-eating could be formed strong enough to call for any extraordinary self-conquest in renouncing it, even suddenly renouncing it. On Saturday you are an opium eater, on Sunday no longer such." [Thomas De Quincey, *Confessions of an English Opium

Eater* (1822), p. 143]

1826   The American Society for the Promotion of Temperance is founded in Boston. By 1833, there are 6,000 local Temperance societies, with more than one million members.

1839-42   The first Opium War. The British force upon China the trade in opium, a trade the Chinese had declared illegal.. [Montagu, op. cit. p. 67]

1840   Benjamin Parsons, and English clergyman, declares: ". . . alcohol stands preeminent as a destroyer. . . . I never knew a person become insane who was not in the habit of taking a portion of alcohol every day." Parsons lists forty-two distinct diseases caused by alcohol, among them inflammation of the brain, scrofula, mania, dropsy, nephritis, and gout. [Quoted in Roueche, op. cit. pp. 87-88]

1841   Dr. Jacques Joseph Moreau uses hashish in treatment of mental patients at the Bicetre.

1842   Abraham Lincoln: "In my judgment, such of us as have never fallen victims, have been spared more from the absence of appetite, than from any mental or moral superiority over those who have. Indeed, I believe, if we take habitual drunkards as a class, their heads and their hearts will bear an advantageous comparison with those of any other class." [Abraham Lincoln, Temperance address, in Roy P. Basler Ed.), *The Collected Works of Abraham Lincoln, Vol. 1, p. 258]

1844   Cocaine is isolated in it's pure form.

1845   A law prohibiting the public sale of liquor is enacted in New York State. It is repealed in 1847.

1847   The American Medical Association is founded.

1852   Susan B. Anthony establishes the Women's State Temperance Society of New York, the first such society formed by and for women. Many of the early feminists, such as Elizabeth Cady Stanton, Lucretia Mott, and Abby Kelly, are also ardent prohibitionists. [Andrew Sinclair, *Era of Excess*, p. 92]

1852   The American Pharmaceutical Association is founded. The Association's 1856 Constitution lists one of its goals as: "To as much as possible restrict the dispensing and sale of medicines to regularly educated druggists and apothecaries. [Quoted in David Musto, *The American Disease*, p. 258]

1856   The Second Opium War. The British, with help from the French, extend their powers to distribute opium in China.

1862   Internal Revenue Act enacted imposing a license fee of twenty dollars on retail liquor dealers, and a tax of one dollar a barrel on beer and twenty cents a gallon on spirits. [Sinclair, op. cit. p 152]

1864   Adolf von Baeyer, a twenty-nine-year-old assistant of Friedrich August Kekule (the discoverer of the molecular structure of benzene) in Ghent, synthesizes barbituric acid, the first barbiturate.

1868   Dr. George Wood, a professor of the theory and practice of medicine at the University of Pennsylvania, president of the American Philosophical Society, and the author of a leading American test, *Treatise on Therapeutics*, describes the pharmacological effects of opium as follows: "A sensation of fullness is felt in the head, soon to be followed by a universal feeling of delicious ease and comfort, with an elevation and expansion of the whole moral and intellectual nature, which is, I think, the most characteristic of its effects. . . . It seems to make the individual, for the time, a better and greater man. . . . The hallucinations, the delirious imaginations of alcoholic intoxication, are, in general, quite wanting. Along with this emotional and intellectual elevation, there is also increased muscular energy; and the capacity to act, and to bear fatigue, is greatly augmented. [Quoted in Musto, op. cit. pp. 71-72]

1869   The Prohibition Party is formed. Gerrit Smith, twice Abolitionist candidate for President, an associate of John Brown, and a crusading prohibitionist, declares: "Our involuntary slaves are set free, but our millions of voluntary slaves still clang their chains. The lot of the literal slave, of him whom others have enslaved, is indeed a hard one; nevertheless, it is a paradise compared with the lot of him who has enslaved himself to alcohol." [Quoted in Sinclair, op. cit. pp. 83-84]

1874   The Woman's Christian Temperance Union is founded in Cleveland. In 1883, Frances Willard a leader of the W.C.T.U. forms the World's Woman's Christian Temperance Union.

1882   The law in the United States, and the world, making "temperance education" a part of the required course in public schools is enacted. In 1886, Congress makes such education mandatory in the District of Columbia, and in territorial, military, and naval schools. By 1900, all the states have similar laws. [Crafts et. al., op. cit. p. 72]

1882   The Personal Liberty League of the United States is founded to oppose the increasing momentum of movements for compulsory abstinence from alcohol. [Catlin, op. cit. p. 114]

Merck Cocaine 1882

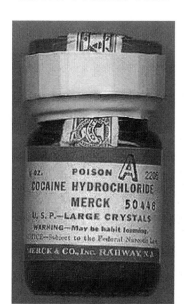

1883   Dr. Theodor Aschenbrandt, a German army physician, secures a supply of pure cocaine from the pharmaceutical firm of Merck, issues it to Bavarian soldiers during their maneuvers, and reports on the beneficial effects of the drug in increasing the soldiers' ability to endure fatigue. [Brecher et. al. op. cit. p. 272]

1884   Sigmund Freud treats his depression with cocaine, and reports feeling "exhilaration and lasting euphoria, which in no way differs from the normal euphoria of the healthy person. . . You perceive an increase in self-control and possess more vitality and capacity for work. . . . In other words, you are simply more normal, and it is soon hard to believe that you are under the influence of a drug." [Quoted in Ernest Jones, *The Life and Work of Sigmund Freud, Vol. 1, p. 82]

1884   Laws are enacted to make anti-alcohol teaching compulsory in public schools in New York State. The following year similar laws are passed in Pennsylvania, with other states soon following suit.

1885   The Report of the Royal Commission on Opium concludes that opium is more like the Westerner's liquor than a substance to be feared and abhorred. [Quoted in Musto, op. cit. p. 29]

1889   The John Hopkins Hospital, in Baltimore, Maryland, is opened. One of its world-famous founders, Dr. William Stewart Halsted, is a morphine addict. He continues to use morphine in large doses throughout his phenomenally successful surgical career lasting until his death in 1922.

1894   The Report of the Indian Hemp Drug Commission, running to over three thousand pages in seven volumes, is published. This inquiry, commissioned by the British government, concluded: "There is no evidence of any weight regarding the mental and moral injuries from the moderate use of these drugs. .. . Moderation does not lead to excess in hemp any more than it does in alcohol. Regular, moderate use of ganja or bhang produces the same effects as moderate and regular doses of whiskey." The commission's proposal to tax bhang is never put into effect, in part, perhaps, because one of the commissioners, an Indian, cautions that Moslem law and Hindu custom forbid "taxing anything that gives pleasure to the poor." [Quoted in Norman Taylor, The pleasant assassin: The story of marihuana, in David Solomon (Ed.) *The Marijuana Papers*, pp. 31-47, p. 41]

1894   Norman Kerr, and English physician and president of the British Society for the study of Inebriety, declares: "Drunkenness has generally been regarded as . . . a sin a vice, or a crime. . . [But] there is now a consensus of intelligent opinion that habitual and periodic drunkenness is often either a symptom or sequel of disease . . . . The victim can no more resist [alcohol] than an man with ague can resist shivering. [Quoted in Roueche, op. cit., pp. 107-108]

1898   Diacetylmorphine (heroin) is synthesized in Germany. It is widely lauded as a "safe preparation free from addiction-forming properties." [Montagu, op. cit. p. 68]

1900   In an address to the Ecumenical Missionary Conference, Rev. Wilbur F. Crafts declares: "No Christian celebration of the completion of nineteen Christian centuries has yet been arranged. Could there be a fitter one than the general adoption, by separate and joint action of the great nations of the world, of the new policy of civilization, in which Great Britain is leading, the policy of prohibition for the native races, in the interest of commerce as well as conscience, since the liquor traffic among child races, even more manifestly than in civilized lands, injures all other trades by producing poverty, disease, and death. Our object, more profoundly viewed, is to create a more favorable environment for the child races that civilized nations are essaying to civilize and Christianize." [Quoted in Crafts, et. al., op. cit., p. 14]

1900   James R. L. Daly, writing in the *Boston Medical and Surgical Journal*, declares: "It [heroin] possesses many advantages over morphine. . . . It is not hypnotic; and there is no danger of acquiring the habit. . . ." [Quoted in Henry H. Lenard et. al. Methadone treatment (letters),*Science*, 179:1078-1079 (March 16), 1973; p. 1079]

1901   The Senate adopts a resolution, introduced by Henry Cabot Lodge, to forbid the sale by American traders of opium and alcohol "to aboriginal tribes and uncivilized races." Theses provisions are later extended to include "uncivilized elements in America itself and in its territories, such as Indians, Alaskans, the inhabitants of Hawaii, railroad workers, and immigrants at ports of entry." [Sinclair, op. cit. p. 33]

1902   The Committee on the Acquirement of the Drug Habit of the American Pharmaceutical Association declares: "If the Chinaman cannot get along without his 'dope,' we can get along without him." [Quoted in ibid, p. 17]

1902   George E. Petty, writing in the *Alabama Medical Journal*, observes: "Many articles have appeared in the medical literature during the last two years lauding this new agent . . . . When we consider the fact that heroin is a morphine derivative . . . it does not seem reasonable that such a claim could be well founded. It is strange that such a claim should mislead anyone or that there should be found among the members of our profession those who would reiterate and accentuate it without first subjecting it to the most critical tests, but such is the fact." [Quoted in Lenard et. al., op. cit. p. 1079]

1903   The composition of Coca-Cola is changed, caffeine replacing the cocaine it contained until this time. {Musto, op. cit. p. 43]
Cocaine is removed from Coca-Cola in 1903.

1904   Charles Lyman, president of the International Reform Bureau, petitions the President of the United States "to induce Great Britain to release China from the enforced opium traffic. . . .We need not recall in detail that China prohibited the sale of opium except as a medicine, until the sale was forced upon that country by Great Britain in the opium war of 1840." [Quoted in Crafts et al., op. cit. p. 230]

1905   Senator Henry W. Blair, in a letter to Rev. Wilbur F. Crafts, Superintendent of the International Reform Bureau: "The temperance movement must include all poisonous substances which create unnatural appetite, and international prohibition is the goal." [Quoted in ibid.]

1906   The first Pure Food and Drug Act becomes law; until its enactment, it was possible to buy, in stores or by mail order medicines containing morphine, cocaine, or heroin, and without their being so labeled.

1906   *Squibb's Material Medical* lists heroin as "a remedy of much value . . . is also used as a mild anodyne and as a substitute for morphine in combating the morphine habit. [Quoted in Lenard et al., op. cit. p. 1079]

1909   The United States prohibits the importation of smoking opium. [Lawrence Kolb, *Drug Addiction*, pp. 145-146]

1910   Dr. Hamilton Wright, considered by some the father of U.S. anti-narcotics laws, reports that American contractors give cocaine to their Negro employees to get more work out of them. [Musto, op. cit. p. 180]

1912   A writer in *Century* magazine proclaims: "The relation of tobacco, especially in the form of cigarettes, and alcohol and opium is a very close one. . . . Morphine is the legitimate consequence of alcohol, and alcohol is the legitimate consequence of tobacco. Cigarettes, drink, opium, is the logical and regular series." And a physician warns: "[There is] no energy more destructive of soul, mind, and body, or more subversive of good morals than the cigarette. The fight against the cigarette is a fight for civilization." [Sinclair, op. cit., p. 180]

1912   The first international Opium Convention meets at

the Hague, and recommends various measures for the international control of the trade in opium. Subsequent Opium Conventions are held in 1913 and 1914.

1912   Phenobarbital is introduced into therapeutics under the trade name of Luminal.

1913   The Sixteenth Amendment, creating the legal authority for federal income tax, is enacted. Between 1870 and 1915, the tax on liquor provides from one-half to two-thirds of the whole of the internal revenue of the United States, amounting, after the turn of the century, to about $200 million annually. The Sixteenth Amendment thus makes possible, just seven years later, the Eighteenth Amendment.

1914   The Harrison Narcotic Act is enacted, controlling the sale of opium and opium derivatives, and cocaine.

1914   Negro leaders join the crusade against alcohol. [Ibid., p. 29]

1916   The *Pharmacopoeia of the United States* drops whiskey and brandy from it's list of drugs. Four years later, American physicians begin prescribing these "drugs" in quantities never before prescribed by doctors.

1917   The president of the American Medical Association endorses national prohibition. The House of Delegates of the Association passes a resolution stating: "Resolved, The American Medical Association opposes the use of alcohol as a beverage; and be it further Resolved, That the use of alcohol as a therapeutic agent should be discourages." By 1928, physicians make an estimated $40,000,000 annually by writing prescriptions for whiskey." [Ibid. p. 61]

1917   The American Medical Association passes a resolution declaring that "sexual continence is compatible with health and is the best prevention of venereal infections," and one of the methods for controlling syphilis is by controlling alcohol. Secretary of the Navy Josephus Daniels prohibits the practice of distributing contraceptives to sailors bound on shore leave, and Congress passes laws setting up "dry and decent zones" around military camps. "Many barkeepers are fined for selling liquor to men in uniform. Only at Coney Island could soldiers and sailors change into the grateful anonymity of bathing suits and drink without molestation from patriotic passers-by." [Ibid. pp. 117-118]

1918   The Anti-Saloon League calls the "liquor traffic" "un-American," pro-German, crime-producing, food-wasting, youth-corrupting, home-wrecking, [and] treasonable." [Quoted in ibid. p. 121]

1919   The Eighteenth (Prohibition) Amendment is added to the U.S. Constitution. It is repealed in 1933. In the same year, violent crime drops two-thirds and does not reach the same levels again until after World War II.

1920   The U.S. Department of Agriculture publishes a pamphlet urging Americans to grow cannabis (marijuana) as a profitable undertaking. [David F. Musto, An historical perspective on legal and medical responses to substance abuse, *Villanova Law Review*, 18:808-817 (May), 1973; p. 816]

1920-1933   The use of alcohol is prohibited in the United States. In 1932 alone, approximately 45,000 persons receive jail sentences for alcohol offenses. During the first eleven years of the Volstead Act, 17,971 persons are appointed to the Prohibition Bureau. 11,982 are terminated "without prejudice," and 1,604 are dismissed for bribery, extortion, theft, falsification of records, conspiracy, forgery, and perjury. [Fort, op. cit. p. 69]

1921   The U.S. Treasury Department issues regulations outlining the treatment of addiction permitted under the Harrison Act. In Syracuse, New York, the narcotics clinic doctors report curing 90 per cent of their addicts. [Lindensmith, *The Addict and the Law*, p. 141]

1921   Thomas S. Blair, M.D., chief of the Bureau of Drug Control of the Pennsylvania Department of Health, publishes a paper in the *Journal of the American Medical Association* in which he characterizes the Indian peyote religion a "habit indulgence in certain cetaceous plants," calls the belief system "superstition" and those who sell peyote "dope vendors," and urges the passage of a bill in Congress that would prohibit the use of peyote among the Indian tribes of the Southwest. He concludes with this revealing plea for abolition: "The great difficulty in suppressing this habit among the Indians arises from the fact that the commercial interests involved in the peyote traffic are strongly entrenched, and they exploit the Indian. . . . Added to this is the superstition of the Indian who believes in the Peyote Church. As soon as an effort is made to suppress peyote, the cry is raised that it is unconstitutional to do so and is an invasion of religious liberty. Suppose the Negros of the South had Cocaine Church!" [Thomas S. Blair, Habit indulgence in certain cetaceous plants among the Indians, *Journal of the American Medical Association*, 76:1033-1034 (April 9), 1921; p. 1034]

1921   Cigarettes are illegal in fourteen states, and ninety-two anti-cigarette bills are pending in twenty-eight states. Young women are expelled from college for smoking cigarettes. [Brecher et al., op. cit. p. 492]

1921   The Council of the American Medical Association refuses to confirm the Associations 1917 Resolution on alcohol. In the first six months after the enactment of the Volstead Act, more than 15,000 physicians and 57,000 druggists and drug manufacturers apply for licenses to prescribe and sell liquor. [Sinclair, op. cit., p. 492]

1921   Alfred C. Prentice, M.D. a member of the Committee

on Narcotic Drugs of the American Medical Association, declares "Public opinion regarding the vice of drug addiction has been deliberately and consistently corrupted through propaganda in both the medical and lay press. . . . The shallow pretense that drug addiction is a 'disease'. . . . has been asserted and urged in volumes of 'literature' by self-styled 'specialists.'" [Alfred C Prentice, The Problem of the narcotic drug addict, *Journal of the American Medical Association*, 76:1551-1556; p. 1553]

1924   The manufacture of heroin is prohibited in the United States.

1925   Robert A. Schless: "I believe that most drug addiction today is due directly to the Harrison Anti-Narcotic Act, which forbids the sale of narcotics without a physician's prescription. . . . Addicts who are broke act as *agent provocateurs* for the peddlers, being rewarded by gifts of heroin or credit for supplies. The Harrison Act made the drug peddler, and the drug peddler makes drug addicts." [Robert A. Schless, The drug addict, *American Mercury*, 4:196-199 (Feb.), 1925; p. 198]

1928   In a nationwide radio broadcast entitled "The Struggle of Mankind Against Its Deadliest Foe," celebrating the second annual Narcotic Education Week, Richmond P. Hobson, prohibition crusader and anti-narcotics propagandist, declares: "Suppose it were announced that there were more than a million lepers among our people. Think what a shock the announcement would produce! Yet drug addiction is far more incurable than leprosy, far more tragic to its victims, and is spreading like a moral and physical scourge. . . . Most of the daylight robberies, daring holdups, cruel murders and similar crimes of violence are now known to be committed chiefly by drug addicts, who constitute the primary cause of our alarming crime wave. Drug addiction is more communicable and less curable that leprosy. . . . Upon the issue hangs the perpetuation of civilization, the destiny of the world, and the future of the human race." [Quoted in Musto, *The American Disease*, p. 191]

1928   It is estimated that in Germany one out of every hundred physicians is a morphine addict, consuming 0.1 grams of the alkaloid or more per day. [Eric Hesse, *Narcotics and Drug Addiction*, p. 41]

1929   About one gallon of denatured industrial in ten is diverted into bootleg liquor. About forty Americans per million die each year from drinking illegal alcohol, mainly as a result of methyl (wood) alcohol poisoning. [Sinclair, op. cit. p. 201]

1930   The Federal Bureau of Narcotics is formed. Many of its agents, including its first commissioner, Harry J. Anslinger, are former prohibition agents.

1935   The American Medical Association passes a resolution declaring that "alcoholics are valid patients." [Quoted in Neil Kessel and Henry Walton, *Alcoholism*, p. 21]

1936   The Pan-American Coffee Bureau is organized to promote coffee use in the U.S. Between 1938 and 1941 coffee consumption increased 20%. From 1914 to 1938 consumption had increased 20%. [Coffee, *Encyclopedia Britannica* (1949), Vol. 5, p. 975A]

1937   Shortly before the Marijuana Tax Act, Commissioner Harry J. Anslinger writes: "How many murders, suicides, robberies, criminal assaults, hold-ups, burglaries, and deeds of maniacal insanity it [marijuana] causes each year, especially among the young, can only be conjectured." [Quoted in John Kaplan, *Marijuana*, p. 92]

1937   The Marijuana Tax Act is enacted. On Oct 8 1937, a Mr. Samuel Caldwell is arrested and begins 4 years hard labor for selling 2 joints.

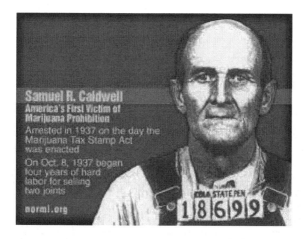

Samuel R. Caldwell
America's First Victim of
Marijuana Prohibition
Arrested in 1937 on the day the
Marijuana Tax Stamp Act
was enacted

On Oct. 8, 1937 began
four years of hard
labor for selling
two joints

norml.org

COLA STATE PEN
1 8 6 9 9

1938   Since the enactment of the Harrison Act in 1914, 25,000 physicians have been arraigned on narcotics charges, and 3,000 have served penitentiary sentences. [Kolb, op. cit. p. 146]

1938   Dr. Albert Hoffman, a chemist at Sandoz Laboratories in Basle, Switzerland, synthesizes LSD. Five years later he inadvertently ingests a small amount of it, and observes and reports effects on himself.

1941   Generalissimo Chiang Kai-shek orders the complete suppression of the poppy; laws are enacted providing the death penalty for anyone guilty of cultivating the poppy, manufacturing opium, or offering it for sale. [Lindensmith, *The Addict and the Law*, 198]

1943   Colonel J. M. Phalen, editor of the *Military Surgeon*, declares in an editorial entitled "The Marijuana Bugaboo": "The smoking of the leaves, flowers, and seeds of Cannabis sativa is no more harmful than the smoking of tobacco. . . . It is hoped that no witch hunt will be instituted in the military service over a problem that does not exist." [Quoted in ibid. p. 234]

1946   According to some estimates there are 40,000,000

opium smokers in China. [Hesse, op. cit. p. 24]

1949   Ludwig von Mises, leading modern free-market economist and social philosopher: "Opium and morphine are certainly dangerous, habit-forming drugs. But once the principle is admitted that is the duty of government to protect the individual against his own foolishness, no serious objections can be advanced against further encroachments. A good case could be made out in favor of the prohibition of alcohol and nicotine. And why limit the governments benevolent providence to the protection of the individual's body only? Is not the harm a man can inflect on his mind and soul even more disastrous than any bodily evils? Why not prevent him from reading bad books and seeing bad plays, from looking at bad paintings and statues and listening to bad music? The mischief done by bad ideologies, surely, is much more pernicious, both for the individual and for the whole society, than that done by narcotic drugs." [Ludwig von Mises, *Human Action*, pp. 728-729]

1951   According to United Nations estimates, there are approximately 200 million marijuana users in the world, the major places being India, Egypt, North Africa, Mexico, and the United States. [Jock Young, *The Drug Takers*, p. 11]

1951   Twenty thousand pounds of opium, three hundred pounds of heroin, and various opium-smoking devices are publicly burned in Canton, China. Thirty-seven opium addicts are executed in the southwest of China. [Margulies, China has no drug problem—why? *Parade*, Oct. 15 1972, p. 22]

1954   Four-fifths of the French people questioned about wine assert that wine is "good for one's health," and one quarter hold that it is "indispensable." It is estimated that a third of the electorate in France receives all or part of its income from the production or sale of alcoholic beverages; and that there is one outlet for every forty- five inhabitants.

[Kessel and Walton, op. cit. pp. 45, 73]

1955   The Prasidium des Deutschen Arztetages declares: "Treatment of the drug addict should be effected in the closed sector of a psychiatric institution. Ambulatory treatment is useless and in conflict, moreover, with principles of medical ethics." The view is quoted approvingly, as representative of the opinion of "most of the authors recommending commitment to an institution," by the World Health Organization in 1962. [World Health Organization, *The Treatment of Drug Addicts*, p. 5]

1955   The Shah of Iran prohibits the cultivation and use of opium, used in the country for thousands of years; the prohibition creates a flourishing illicit market in opium. In 1969 the prohibition is lifted, opium growing is resumed under state inspection, and more than 110,000 persons receive opium from physicians and pharmacies as "registered addicts." [Henry Kamm, They shoot opium smugglers in Iran, but . . ." *The New York Times Magazine*, Feb. 11, 1973, pp. 42-45]

1956   The Narcotics Control Act in enacted; it provides the death penalty, if recommended by the jury, for the sale of heroin to a person under eighteen by one over eighteen. [Lindensmith, *The Addict and the Law*, p. 26]

1958   Ten percent of the arable land in Italy is under viticulture; two million people earn their living wholly or partly from the production or sale of wine. [Kessel and Walton, op. cit., p. 46]

1960   The United States report to the United Nations Commission on Narcotic Drugs for 1960 states: "There were 44,906 addicts in the United States on December 31, 1960 . . ." [Lindensmith, *The Addict and The Law*, p. 100]

1961   The United Nations' "Single Convention on Narcotic Drugs of 10 March 1961" is ratified. Among the obligations of the signatory states are the following: "Art. 42. Known users of drugs and persons charges with an offense under this Law may be committed by an examining magistrate to a nursing home. . . . Rules shall be also laid down for the treatment in such nursing homes of unconvicted drug addicts and dangerous alcoholics." [Charles Vaille, A model law for the application of the Single Convention on Narcotic Drugs, 1961, *United Nations Bulletin on Narcotics*, 21:1-12 (April-June), 1961]

1963   Tobacco sales total $8.08 billion, of which $3.3 billion go to federal, state, and local taxes. A news release from the tobacco industry proudly states: "Tobacco products pass across sales counters more frequently than anything else–except money." [Tobacco: After publicity surge Surgeon General's Report seems to have little enduring effect, *Science*, 145:1021-1022 (Sept. 4), 1964; p. 1021]

1964   The British Medical Association, in a Memorandum of Evidence to the Standing Medical Advisory Committee's Special Sub- committee on Alcoholism, declares: "We feel that in some very bad cases, compulsory detention in hospital offer the only hope of successful treatment. . . . We believe that some alcoholics would welcome compulsory removal and detention in hospital until treatment is completed." [Quoted in Kessel and Walton, op. cit. p. 126]

1964   An editorial in *The New York Times* calls attention to the fact that "the Government continues to be the tobacco industry's biggest booster. The Department of Agriculture lost $16 million in supporting the price of tobacco in the last fiscal year, and stands to loose even more because it has just raised the subsidy that tobacco growers will get on their 1964 crop. At the same time, the Food for Peace program is getting rid of surplus stocks of tobacco abroad." [Editorial, Bigger agricultural subsidies. . .even more for tobacco, *The New York Times*, Feb. 1, 1964, p. 22]

1966   Sen. Warren G. Magnuson makes public a program, sponsored by the Agriculture Department, to subsidize "attempts to increase cigarette consumption abroad. . . . The Department is paying to stimulate cigarette smoking in a travelogue for $210,000 to subsidize cigarette commercials in Japan, Thailand, and Austria." An Agriculture Department spokesman corroborates that "the two programs were prepared under a congressional authorization to expand overseas markets for U.S. farm commodities." [Edwin B. Haakinsom, Senator shocked at U.S. try to hike cigarette use abroad, *Syracuse Herald-American*, Jan. 9, 1966, p. 2]

1966   Congress enacts the "Narcotics Addict Rehabilitation Act", inaugurating a federal civil commitment program for addicts.

1966   C. W. Sandman, Jr. chairman of the New Jersey Narcotic Drug Study Commission, declares that LSD is "the greatest threat facing the country today . . . more dangerous than the Vietnam War." [Quoted in Brecher et al., op. cit. p. 369]

1967   New York State's "Narcotics Addiction Control Program" goes into effect. It is estimated to cost $400 million in three years, and is hailed by Governor Rockefeller as the "start of an unending war . . ." Under the new law, judges are empowered to commit addicts for compulsory treatment for up to five years. [Murray Schumach, Plan for addicts will open today: Governor hails start, *The New York Times*, April 1, 1967]

1967   The tobacco industry in the United States spends an estimated $250 million on advertising smoking. [Editorial, It depends on you, *Health News* (New York State), 45:1 (March), 1968]

1968   The U.S. tobacco industry has gross sales of $8

billion. Americans smoke 544 billion cigarettes. [Fort, op. cit. p. 21]

1968   Canadians buy almost 3 billion aspirin tablets and approximately 56 million standard doses of amphetamines. About 556 standard doses of barbiturates are also produced or imported for consumption in Canada. [Canadian Government's Commission of Inquiry, *The Non-Medical Uses of Drugs*, p. 184

1968   Six to seven percent of all prescriptions written under the British National Health Service are for barbiturates; it is estimated that about 500,000 British are regular users. [Young, op. cit. p. 25]

1968   Brooklyn councilman Julius S. Moskowitz charges that the work of New York City's Addiction Services Agency, under its retiring Commissioner, Dr. Efren Ramirez, was a "fraud," and that "not a single addict has been cured." [Charles G. Bennett, Addiction agency called a "fraud," *New York Times*, Dec. 11, 1968, p. 47]

Millions are made from Barbiturates like Seconal, and overdoses surge during the 1960's and 70's.

1969   U.S. production and value of some medical chemicals: barbiturates: 800,000 pounds, $2.5 million; aspirin (exclusive of salicylic acid) 37 million pounds, value "withheld to avoid disclosing figures for individual producers"; salicylic acid: 13 million pounds, $13 million; tranquilizers: 1.5 million pounds, $7 million. [*Statistical Abstracts of the United States*, 1971 92nd Annual Edition, p. 75]

1969   The parents of 6,000 secondary-level students in Clifton, New Jersey, are sent letters by the Board of Education asking permission to conduct saliva tests on their children to determine whether or not they use marijuana. [Saliva tests asked for Jersey youths on marijuana use, *New York Times*, Apr. 11, 1969, p. 12]

1970   Dr. Albert Szent-Gyorgyi, Nobel Laureate in Medicine and Physiology, in reply to being asked what he would do if he were twenty today: "I would share with my classmates rejection of the whole world as it is–all of it. Is there any point in studying and work? Fornication–at least that is something good. What else is there to do? Fornicate and take drugs against the terrible strain of idiots who govern the world." [Albert Szent-Gyorgyi, in *The New York Times*, Feb. 20, 1970, quoted in Mary Breastead, *Oh! Sex Education!*, p. 359]

1971   President Nixon declares that "America's Public Enemy No. 1 is drug abuse." In a message to Congress, the President calls for the creation of a Special Action Office of Drug Abuse Prevention. [The New Public Enemy No. 1, *Time*, June 28, 1971, p. 18]

1971   On June 30, 1971, President Cvedet Sunay of Turkey decrees that all poppy cultivation and opium production will be forbidden beginning in the fall of 1972. [Patricia M Wald et al. (Eds.), *Dealing with Drug Abuse*, p. 257]

1972   Myles J. Ambrose, Special Assistant Attorney General of the United States: "As of 1960, the Bureau of Narcotics estimated that we had somewhere in the neighborhood of 55,000 addicts . . . they estimate now the figure is 560,000. [Quoted in *U.S. News and World Report*, April 3, 1972, p. 38]

1972   The Bureau of Narcotics and Dangerous Drugs proposes restricting the use of barbiturates on the ground that they "are more dangerous than heroin." [Restrictions proposed on barbiturate sales, *Syracuse Herald-Journal*, Mar 16, 1972, p. 32]

1972   The house votes 366 to 0 to authorize "a $1 billion, three-year federal attack on drug abuse." [$1 billion voted for drug fight, *Syracuse Herald-Journal*, March 16, 1972, p. 32]

1972   At the Bronx house of corrections, out of a total of 780 inmates, approximately 400 are given tranquilizers such as Valium, Elavil, Thorazine, and Librium. "'I think they [the inmates] would be doing better without some of the medication,' said Capt. Robert Brown, a correctional officer. He said that in a way the medications made his job harder . . . rather than becoming calm, he said, an inmate who had become addicted to his medication 'will do anything when he can't get it.'" [Ronald Smothers, Muslims: What's behind the violence, *The New York Times*, Dec. 26, 1972, p. 18]

1972   In England, the pharmacy cost of heroin is $.04 per grain (60 mg.), or $.00067 per mg. In the United States, the street price is $30 to $90 per grain, or $.50 or $1.50 per mg. [Wald et al. (Eds.) op. cit. p. 28]

Heroin was provided on prescription in what was known as 'The British System'. Only a few hundred opiate dependent users receive it this way today.

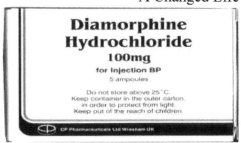

Diamorphine Hydrochloride
100mg
for Injection BP
5 ampoules

Do not store above 25°C.
Keep container in the outer carton.
in order to protect from light.
Keep out of the reach of children.

CP Pharmaceuticals Ltd Wrexham UK

1973   A nationwide Gallop poll reveals that 67 percent of the adults interviewed "support the proposal of New York Governor Nelson Rockefeller that all sellers of hard drugs be given life imprisonment without possibility of parole." [George Gallup, Life for pushers, *Syracuse Herald-American*, Feb. 11, 1973]

1973   Michael R. Sonnenreich, Executive Director of the National Commission on Marijuana and Drug Abuse, declares: "About our years ago we spent a total of $66.4 million for the entire federal effort in the drug abuse area. . . . This year we have spent $796.3 million and the budget estimates that have been submitted indicate that we will exceed the $1 billion mark. When we do so, we become, for want of a better term, a drug abuse industrial complex.: [Michael R. Sonnenreich, Discussion of the Final Report of the National Commission on Marijuana and Drug Abuse, *Villanova Law Review*, 18:817-827 (May), 1973; p. 818]

1972   Operation Intercept. All vehicles returning from Mexico are checked by Nixon's order. Long lines occur and, as usual no dent is made in drug traffic.

1977   The Joint Committee of the New York Bar Association concludes that the Rockefeller drug laws, the toughest in the nation, have had no effect in reducing drug use but have clogged the courts and the criminal justice system to the point of gridlock.

1981   Congress amends the 1878 Posse Comitatus Act, which forbids the armed forces to enforce civil law, so that the military could provide surveillance planes and ships for interdiction purposes. (prevent illegal entry: to prevent somebody or something from entering a country illegally. Patrols will be increased along the border to interdict smugglers.)

1982   President Ronald Reagan declares "War on Drugs." On October 14, 1982 President Ronald Reagan declared illicit drugs to be a threat to U.S. national security.

1984   U.S. busts 10,000 pounds of marijuana on farms in Mexico. The seizures, made on five farms in an isolated section of Chihuahua state, suggest a 70 percent increase in estimates that total U.S. consumption was 13,000 to 14,000 tons in 1982. Furthermore, the seizures add up to nearly eight times the 1300 tons that officials had calculated Mexico produced in 1983. [the San Francisco Chronicle, Saturday, November 24, 1984]

1985   Pentagon spends $40 million on interdiction to prevent drug smuggling. By 1990, the General Accounting Office will report that the military's efforts have had no discernible impact on the flow of drugs.

1986   The Communist Party boss, Boris Yeltsin said that the Moscow school system is rife with drug addiction, drunkenness and principals that take bribes. He said that drug addiction has become such a problem that there are 3700 registered addicts in Moscow. [The San Francisco Chronicle, Sept. 22, 1986, p. 12]

1992   AIVL – Australian Intravenous League -who then changed the name to Australian Injecting and Illicit drug users League, of which it is currently known, was formally constituted in 1992 although they began in 1988. Having grown to be one of the world largest user orgs, AIVL is the national user organization, with chapters in every Australian state. Government funded and peer run.

2002   The Swedish Drug User Union is born, Swedish Drug Users Union Hep C campaign.   (SDUU) and grows quickly adding many local chapters, the first one being Stockholm (S. The Swedish Drug Users Union (SDUU) is an NGO and was founded in October 2002 by drug users associated to the Swedish Opiate Substitution Treatment programs. They fight hard against Swedish conservatism in drug policy to ensure the voice and views of the drug user are included in every issue that affects their lives, following the user activist mantra 'Nothing About Us Without Us'.

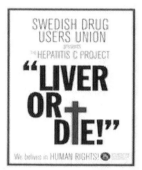

2008   INPUD (International Network for People who Use Drugs) is formally launched on International Drug Users day Nov 1st 2008 at the premises of the Danish Drug Users Union, where around 100 international activists came from around 30 countries. INPUD was established to represent the interests of drug users on the world stage, especially those who encounter human rights violations, are affected by blood borne viruses and encounter discrimination simply because of their personal drug use.

2012   The Netherlands' begins its crackdown on its much loved cannabis 'coffee shop' system'. Three areas begin a pilot program on May 1st, 2012 of excluding foreigners (except Belgians' and Germans') from buying dope in Amsterdam's traditional Coffee Shops and introduce a 'Weed Pass' allowing only 2000 Dutch customers per establishment. The experiment is to roll out across the country   on   Jan.   1st,   2013   if   successful. http://www.coffeeshopsamsterdam.com/home.html

*

Since the preceding data was compiled, research clearly shows that heroin and opioid addiction have become an epidemic in the past 15 years.   The skyrocket rise of methamphetamine is now ruinous.

LIFE STORIES

LIFE STORY #1

Male, 25 years of age

I was born in Paragould, Arkansas.   I had two loving parents.   They got a divorce when I was just four years old.   My dad worked a lot and in his spare time he drove stock cars.   He was my best friend.   When my mom and my dad got a divorce I was too young to understand what was happening.   My mom always took the best care she could of me.

When she got remarried things got bad.   The only good thing that occurred was I gained a brother.   My mom and her new husband moved a lot and she was the only one to work.   My dad moved a lot too and a stable home is something I never had except when I lived with my pepaw.   My mom's husband did drugs and was not a good role model and he went to jail a lot.   Seeing all this made me see who I didn't want to become like.

I went to see my dad every summer and Christmas break when I didn't go to school.   I always had fun when I went there.   I skate-boarded a lot when I turned fourteen to ease my hurt that I was feeling from not seeing my dad as much and from what my mom was going through with her husband.   When I was fifteen, they finally divorced.   I was glad.   My mom and I started to get a relationship back.   I hadn't seen my dad for three years but we talked all the time.   I still felt hurt but I enjoyed him calling me.

I was in Junior High now in Paragould.   I had gained some friends.   One day when I was sixteen I was talking to my dad.   I was smoking weed at this time. I was at my friend's house and my dad sounded troubled but I didn't think anything about it.   He said, "Son, I love you.   Always remember that."   I said, "I love you, too.   I'll call you tomorrow."   What I didn't know was that was going to be the last time I could say I loved him.   The next morning I called him over and over.   My mom called and told me to get home.

She told me, "I'm so sorry, son."   I kept asking what was wrong.   She said, "Your dad died."   My heart shattered.   I was so broken.   The whole time that we were headed to Shreveport, Louisiana, I did nothing except cry.   This is where things got real bad.   After the funeral I just wanted to stop the pain.   I started pushing my mom away.   I blamed it all on God and her.   I cussed God out and I didn't want anything to do with Him.   I skipped school a lot and my drug habit increased.   I got highly addicted to xanax and cough syrup.   I would take any pill that would make me feel anything but hurting.   My mom couldn't stop me and when she tried I just fought back harder. One day I took a lot of anxiety meds and I tried to slit my throat but my aunt put her hand in the way and I cut her hand.   My mom was so worried.   I had court the next day for skipping school.   My mom told the judge what happened.   He decided to send me to

Bridgeway for help with my suicide.   It didn't help my drug use though.   As soon as I got out it was back to pills and weed.   When I turned eighteen I tried meth. I liked it too much.   I dropped out of school and this new habit picked up and my life spiraled down even more.   I went to go pick up my (now) step-brother, Tyler.   A fight broke out over ten dollars.   I saw a man get murdered.   It haunts me still.

My mom met a nice guy who she is now married to. He tried to help me but I didn't listen.   I was beyond human repair.   As the months went by so did my life. The only thing I knew was sex, drugs, and rock-n-roll. Every girl I got involved with, I wrecked their lives.   I used them...sex, money and their home.   Wherever I went chaos and misery followed.   I started shooting up.   Life really hit it's all time low now.   I stole, lied, hustled, and did anything for my next shot.   My nana talked me into going into a rehab so I did.   But not for my benefit, it was for hers.   I stayed for a couple of months but I still got high there.   I would go to town when I was there for three months to pick up drugs.   My habit never stopped, just slowed down.   I left after I got fed up with it.   I went to Shreveport to stay with my uncle.   He cared a lot for me and helped me anyway he could.   My papa let me work with him to earn some money but drugs did not leave my mind and they were easy to get and find.   It's sad, the thing I said I never wanted to be, turned out to be the only thing I was good at-that was being a junkie.   And I was being the best one I could be.   My uncle tried to get me help but I moved back to Paragould, Arkansas.

I was now twenty-two and in and out of jail and suicide hospitals.   I was so lost and broken.   I got back around my junkie acquaintances.   I fell back to drugs and this time it got worse.   I had nowhere to go until my aunt in Medical Lake, Washington took me in. I did good for a little while until I found out marijuana was legal so I bought all I could get.   Then I met a guy who introduced me to heroin.   I was hooked instantly.   I would borrow money from my aunt and my nana.   Nothing helped my pain.   I was just looking for a cure to fill the empty hole in my heart. Everything I did got me nowhere.   My aunt got fed up and kicked me out.   I couldn't blame her.

I moved back to Paragould, Arkansas.   I got back into the old people I hung with.   I got tired of it.   I was hopeless, no money, no clothes, and no hope.   I tried to end my life by overdosing but never succeeded.   I showed up at my mom's house so broken.   I asked for her to get me help.   Her husband told her to help me. She took me to St. Bernard's and got me into the mental hospital.   They knew I wasn't crazy.   I just needed help with drug addiction.

I called God's New Life.   It took four days of calling to show I really wanted the help.   I got accepted.   My mom was excited about bringing me.   I didn't know what to think.   I finally arrived to what saved my life. It is Jesus Christ!   Coming to know Christ is the greatest thing I have ever done.   The only one who made me feel worthy and loved even with my faults. It's more than just coming off drugs.   I'm learning how to cope, love, be loved, deal with my issues, and accept what has happened.   He chose me and forgave me.

I don't know what God has planned for me but I know it's going to be beyond what I could imagine.   Jesus healed me and my relationships with my family.   He has moved mountains I never thought could be moved. I still am learning more about Him and I don't want to stop.   With God you can't stop-you have to always be ready to help and serve for Him when He wants you to. It's no longer about me.   It's about what I can do for God to glorify Him.   I love Jesus and I am so thankful for Him saving me.   I give Him the glory for all He is and will do for me.   His love is unfailing.   If God is for you, who can be against you?

*

Wow!   What a change!   That's what I'm talking about.   When God shows up on the scene, He can take a broken life and apply that instantly bonding krazy glue and you are fixed!

This young man just had to be led in the right direction.   God was dealing with him, leading him, talking to him and he didn't even realize it.   "Make that call, make that call, call them again"-until God's New Life graciously took him in.   There is a song I absolutely love titled, "He Was There All The Time". God had been there patiently waiting, calling this man.   When you have tried everything else, try God. He's been waiting at the end of the line just for you.

This young man had been hurting for so long.   Lost in a world filled with Satan's crowd that were all too willing to introduce him to ways that would help him to ease the pain of his father's death.   Everything but the name of Jesus Christ.   No, the Devil doesn't want you to know that name, hear that name or speak that name.   When you call on Jesus, Satan must flee.   He slithers back to his darkness away from the redemptive and justifying light of Almighty God.

You know, this man sounds like he had family that loved him, took him in, really cared about his welfare.   But the drugs had such a hold on him, he consistently took advantage of the love his family had for him.   I have always heard that love cures all. But that is not true in cases of drug addiction that has gotten to the worst stages.   Family or friends can love a person silly but that won't break that craving.   The drugs infiltrate every nook and cranny of one's body-the brain, the blood, the muscles, the bones, the very heart.   The tentacles wrap around the very sinew of the body and squeeze with a deadly grip.   So even though *people's* love cannot cure all, there is a kind of love that can. That unchanging, all encompassing, completely overwhelming, sweet, tender love of God.   Isn't it wonderful?

I heard the testimony of Bro. Loren Larson, a now evangelist for God.   He was once a drug addict.   He testified that he checked into a motel room and began drinking and shooting up drugs with the full intent to just die.   But during the night, a force woke him from his deadly stupor.   This force walked boldly, forcefully, and unafraid right into that hotel room, amid the needles lying in the floor, right through the middle of the whiskey bottles scattered around the room.   That power called his name. Loren Larson woke up to hear a preacher on the television he had left turned on.   This preacher was telling him about Jesus and how to be saved.   The preacher seemed to be talking directly to him. There was an unseen but very real power, an unexplainable force calling to him, leading him to his knees by his bedside.   His obstinate spirit broke under the power of God and he began to sob, great tears of grief, sorrow, brokenhearted before God. Loren Larson prayed the sinner's prayer and received Christ into his heart.   He was instantly changed from a drug addict on the verge of death to a man on fire for God!

God is not intimidated by needles, silver spoons, whiskey bottles, or any kind of drug paraphernalia. He will never be unequipped to handle any unseemly, unsightly, disgraceful, depths of the gutter situation you have gotten yourself into.   I can ASSURE you that God is able to take the worst situation possible and pull you out of it and set you on higher ground if you are willing to grasp His hand when He extends it to you.

Our young man in this life story has surely felt that same drawing power.   The force that cannot be explained with mortal words.   Each of us who are saved by the grace of God recognize that voice.   We know the shepherd who leads us.   He said, "My sheep know my voice." Yes Lord, I hear. Woe to the person whom Jesus calls and they refuse to heed His voice. What a disastrous mistake to pass up an opportunity to have the riches of Heaven and a precious Savior willing to die for us to cover our sin with His blood sacrifice.

Thankfully, this young man listened to God's call. Let us pray that he never strays from the will of God in his life. What a tremendous testimony this man can give to many that are sinking just like he was. He will do a great work for God!

LIFE STORY #2

Female, 31 years of age

On March 15, 1986 I was born in Memphis, Tennessee at a low income based hospital that my mother worked at.   After ten long hours of labor in the same room as thirteen other women in labor and considering it was first come-first serve, I arrived.

My dad worked for the telephone company in West Memphis, Arkansas where I vaguely remember living but I know my parents worked hard and took very good care of me.   We moved when I was four to Jacksonville, Arkansas where my dad was transferred and I began kindergarten there in a small trailer where we were only taught to play and color.   My brother was born two years after me on February 18th.   We were and still are inseparable.   He plays a major role in my life story as we grow older.

So after the year in Jacksonville, we moved to Jonesboro and that's where we stayed.   I can't say one thing bad about my childhood.   My parents, to this day, are still married going on thirty-six years and as I move on with the "troubled years", they have always been there.   I began kindergarten in Jonesboro and was so far behind seeing as all I had learned was to play and color, I began "Hooked on Phonics".   When I had my first day, they were taking *an SAT test for kindergarten and I felt so far behind, stupid actually.   That was my first encounter of rejection.   Special classes, new kid, etc.   I wasn't slow or had trouble learning.   I just really hadn't been taught.   So as the year continued I picked up and caught up with everyone else and life was back to normal.   My mother got a job at the school me and my brother were attending so I had a lot of help and loved having her there.   I was a straight A student and throughout elementary I was an excellent student. My parents started getting me involved in softball and clogging at age five and I traveled all over dancing and playing ball until I was eighteen.   I was very passionate about both activities and stayed plugged into them constantly.   Win, win, win is all I knew. That mindset was instilled in me at a young age and carried on into my mess, which wasn't good.   I clogged for Southern All-Stars out of Jonesboro that started as once a year recitals and led to competitions every weekend with Showstoppers and eventually opened up for shows in Branson, Missouri.   This was when I wasn't in school.   Always in the limelight it seemed but that was what I thought was normal. Along with clogging, I had softball in the summer, every weekend tournaments and two-three nights a week our team traveled to high school championships.*

Now, I'm not bragging whatsoever.   I just want to kind of lay a foundation of why I believe some things ended up as they did.   In the midst of all the activities I was involved in, I always was in church.   I attended Sunday School, church, VBS, summer camps.   I loved it.   I am grateful my parents chose to keep us there.

They were and still are believers. At age seven one night a neighbor invited me to VBS at night and I was led to the Lord. I remember that tugging on my heart and know I did not want to go to Hell. That year I went to a Heaven's Gates, Hell's Flames and it changed my life. That play made me realize at that young age that Heaven and Hell were real and I was going to live for the Lord. Maybe I was scared of Hell but whatever it took I know I gave my heart to the Lord.

As I continued growing up I stayed very involved and was a good kid. When I entered the 7th grade I had made cheerleading and hung out with the "cool kids". My heart was big though. I had friends of all ages, all colors, all social statuses. I was friends with everyone and never judged someone. Being that way, I was in homecoming every year until I graduated (again, the limelight) and started feeling held to a standard from friends and parents. Being up in everything, I started wearing a mask. And slowly started to change who I truly was. I fell in love for the first time in 7th grade with the baseball star of the school. He was in 10th grade and was quiet the guy. He never did drugs or alcohol, loved the Lord and stayed focused on his future. We were crazy about one another but there was one problem- his family did not agree with our age difference. My parents were fine with it. It was young innocent love but his parents weren't going along with it. So we sneaked around and again I felt rejection. He eventually became a senior and was so good at baseball that he got drafted to the New York Mets, second round.   I felt very cool but that all came to an end.   He moved on to much bigger and better things and I was left in the small town wishing it would have worked.   Felt rejected.   So after all the innocence, I decided I was going to stop wearing those masks for everyone and let loose, have some fun and the story truly begins.

At age sixteen I began hanging out with older kids from Jonesboro High.   They were much more wild than my school mates at my usual school and I fit in. I started dating guys that partied.   So I started partying too.   I smoked cigarettes, LOVED pot and took pills occasionally.   Of course, I drank too.   That continued for a year and at seventeen I started dating a guy who was what I would call a modern day hippie. He had been a best friend for years but we lost touch when he got into dropping acid, mushrooms, weird stuff at the time but as I began to party it started to be acceptable to me.   So we dated and I began to partake.   I began to turn into someone I was totally against.   I started wearing hippie clothes, dreaded my hair, smoking pot before school and on the weekends, following Widespread Panic, making grilled cheese sandwiches in the parking lot of shows and selling them as a cover for all the pot and mushrooms my boyfriend was selling out of the car.   I remember tripping "shrooms", going to a Panic show and the entire coliseum was like a video game I had played with my brother when I was younger.   I bagged "molly" hours prior to shows for a lot of money and that's what I did for a crew of people.   There was a lot of things that went on I had no clue about, later to *find out I'm glad I didn't.*

Of course, thankfully, that only went on for about a year and I truly believe the Lord saved me then because somehow I got back into school.   I did quit cheering but still played ball and chilled out on the "heavy" drugs, smoked pot still and drank at parties but ended up my senior year transferring to Jonesboro High because I could leave school at noon and work . I ended up getting voted to be in the high school pageant and won!   After that I stayed steady on my behavior and applied for Toni & Guy Hairdressing Academy in Dallas, Texas.   I wanted to do something great and make people feel good about themselves so I was accepted and when I graduated high school with a 3.8 grade point in August of 2005, off to Dallas I went to start a new glamorous life.   I had obtained a new boyfriend of course by then who was in college at A-State and was in a fraternity which I loved but he agreed we could date from a distance so I went to school in Dallas six days a week and drove home every weekend to see him.   Crazy.   As you can see, men were a big problem that I tended to revolve my life around.   When I graduated there in Dallas I missed a huge opportunity to work for Toni & Guy Company because I had to get back home for a relationship in Jonesboro.   So I started doing hair in Jonesboro. Eventually I was single again but extremely prosperous in my business.   By 2007, I had made $70,000 after taxes and had a clientele of people waiting weeks to get their hair done.   It was probably the most proud of myself I had ever been to this day I think.

I continued to keep a pretty clean nose, pot and pills only but maintained. In 2008, I received a phone call from D., a guy I had been infatuated with from a small town of McGehee, Arkansas where my dad's side of the family lived.   When I was little, every summer I would go to McGehee to visit and he was the most handsome, coolest man I had ever seen but was way too cool for growing up.   He hung with the older kids and always had an older girlfriend.   Apparently though he saw something in me because on my twenty-first birthday he had heard it was my birthday and just wanted to wish me happy birthday and see how I was.   You would have thought I won the lottery the way I lit up. He called!   So as I'm sure you all could guess we started dating.   Business at the salon was good and D. was an offshore oil rig worker so he worked three weeks on the rig and three weeks at home.   So I managed to pile up all my clients in a three week span so I could be off when he was off and travel down to McGehee to party and hang out with him every second I could get.   I was madly in love with him.   He had the house, the money, the cars, the life style I thought was what I wanted.

So we both drank a lot which really had never been my thing but in a little country town that's what we did. Anything I wanted he gave and did for me.   I thought this is it, I made it through the crappy relationships and finally I was with the one.   I remember one Christmas I was at his mom's and she said you are what we've been praying for!   Finally, parents approval and all I had dreamed.   Honestly it was a big party most of the time but I thought I was happy. I thought I knew myself and him but unfortunately I was wrong.   Six months went by and one night while I was there visiting him we went to his mom's and no one was there.   There were heart shaped plates, candles, pizza and wine.   Funny, but I thought how sweet.   As we sat down and ate he fell out of his chair. I laughed and said, "Get up, goofy", but no, he was on one knee and opened a box, shaking to death, with a three carat diamond ring and said, "K., will you marry me?" I was so overwhelmed at first by the gynormous ring in front of me.   But then I realized he just proposed and, of course, I said, "Yes!"   I cried like a baby and called my parents.   They knew and were thrilled I'm sure thinking K.'s getting married and will be taken care of.   We proceeded to the country club where all his friends were ready to celebrate.   I felt so special and was ready to begin a new life.

We continued our routine of three weeks together and three weeks apart which at times started becoming difficult for me.   The times we were together were a lot of blur because of the alcohol and pills.   But was justified by he couldn't do them while working but when he was home he was allowed to let loose.   The problem with that was he was made to take a break on the use but life stayed the same for me and the use of pills became everyday.   I turned to them when I was lonely, tired, angry, sad-any excuse and that solved the problem.   I thought I could manage but I was wrong.   We had set a date, September 21st, 2008.   I eventually closed my hair booth in Jonesboro and moved to McGehee.   Our house was there and some of my family there.   I began to go to meetings out of town with him when he was home in Houston and Biloxi.   I remember one trip to Biloxi we had finished his meeting and decided to stay a few extra days with a friend of his and just hang out.   Of course, party, hit up the casinos, go to the beach but that was far from what happened.   We got up that morning and his friend pulled out some aluminum foil and proceeded to pull out crystal meth.   I had done A LOT of drugs by then in my life, A LOT, but had never even seen meth.   To me it was a trashy drug.   Everyone I had seen on it looked sick and miserable.   And I was always partaking in "happy drugs".   So I thought surely D. won't do this but the guy passed the foil to him and he smoked it like this wasn't his first rodeo. After he hit it he passed it to me.   I played cool and before I knew it I had hit it too.   Numerous times!   I remember thinking, " Wow, do I know this man I'm about to marry?"

We had never even spoke of meth and all of a sudden I was higher than a birds butt.   I remember walking outside and sitting on the porch and cried.   I know now it was the Holy Spirit conviction.   I couldn't believe I went there.   So of course, we stayed up days and did more but when we spent all of our money and it was time to go home, I sat with a fifth of vodka on the side of a pool trying to get drunk to come down off the dope.   Never again we agreed but that didn't stand either.   Back to reality we went-he left for work and there I was.   I began working at a salon in McGehee and fortunately accumulated a good clientele.   So on to meeting new people and settling down to a town of three thousand maybe, if that, from the city of seventy-five thousand.   We moved into the house on the farm.   It was his parent's when he was little, right out in the middle of a cotton field.

Now just a few years prior I was living in a seven-hundred square foot apartment in Dallas.   Major culture shock.   I remember one day I got all dressed up with cute tan knee boots and a dress from Francesca's Collections which I forgot to tell about in the early years when I was nineteen.   I was hired for a boutique (along with hair as I started out my first year) at Francesca's Collections.   After a few months of sales associate I was asked to travel and open stores as a traveling manager.   I traveled to thirteen states that year opening twenty stores for the company.   It was an amazing once in a lifetime deal but of course I got lonely being gone all the time and truly wanted to pursue my cosmetology career.   Anywho, back to McGehee, so I went to wash some dishes, all ready to go to town and I had no hot water.   So I called D.'s mom and said, "There's no hot water here."   She said, "You see that big white tank behind the house toward the field? Walk out to it, if it says zero, there's no propane and I'll have to call and have them fill it." WHAT?   My goodness, so here I go to the tank, looked up at God and said, "What am I doing?"   I guess a form of doubt was setting in.

So there were months of planning a wedding which my mother did every bit of.   I was and still am very easy going and didn't care much about planning all the details.   I got my dress (a couture gown) in

January.   A beautiful, expensive gown and over the months my parents ended up paying twenty-five thousand dollars out of their retirement to make sure I had the most wonderful day of my life.   And it was. But the night of the rehearsal dinner in Eureka Springs (where we would wed in a complete glass chapel in the middle of the woods-it was beautiful), I did not abide by the rules of not sleeping with the groom before we wed and surprise! I got pregnant the night before I was married.

So, on to honeymoon in Cancun, Mexico.   I got sick the first night I was there and stayed sick the entire trip.   When we got back to the airport in the States I went straight to the hospital to find out I was pregnant!   The trip was supposed to be fun and I wanted at least a year to enjoy being married but the Lord thought otherwise.   That is a whole lot to have on your plate, married and pregnant the first year.   I decided to stay in McGehee.   We could have moved to Jonesboro seeing as my husband was gone working six months out of the year and I could have been where my mom and my doctor was, but I had already started a new life there.

I completely quit everything I was doing-drugs, smoking and drinking when I found out I was having a baby.   I can't say that for my husband.   Assuming he was scared and not ready, he continued to party and hang out late hours into the night.   The big problem started one day when I went to use his phone.   I saw a text to a past girlfriend telling her he still loved her. I was crushed! So instantly the fighting began.   At first it was denial and arguing, then more time away from home.   I remember sitting up at night waiting in the front yard for headlights to come down the road.   I remember so strongly the begging I would do to God in the pitch black of night asking him to just please fix this and let D. love me and his son.   Of course, he'd show up and talk that talk and I'd forgive him but inside I began to harbor a lot of really bad angry feelings.   I just stuffed them away and truly didn't want to know what else he was doing.   The less I knew the better is how I began to think.   All I wanted was to have a normal family before our son was born.

The fighting continued though and before I knew it everyone was involved on both sides of the families. It was all bad!   We tried to play house for months, picking out baby stuff, decorating his room, but after the nine months of lying to one another what I thought we had really was lost.   On June 11, 2009, I gave birth to our son.   I had a c-section.   Because of D.'s job (he had to go back to work for three weeks), I agreed to be induced three days before my due date so D. could be there.   Most of our life revolved around his work schedule but considering that was our bread and butter, that came first.   He left three days after our son was born to work so it was me and the baby and thankfully, my mom.   Considering I had a c-section with seventeen stitches I needed help with the new baby.   My mom was wonderful and so was that precious baby boy.   The only problem was seeing as I had surgery, I was prescribed percocets.   My doctor was in Jonesboro four hours away so he gave me one-

hundred and sixty "just in case" every two weeks for a month and a half and I formed a habit.   I could take them and get all that was needed done plus they helped me stay energized for those long baby nights. Before I knew it I needed them to function.   How selfish and unfair to my son.

One thing is, he was never neglected and he was always first no matter what at this point.   When D. would come home we had good times as a little family but we were taking pills.   It became a habit every time he was home, drugs, but still on the outside a normal functioning family.   Behind closed doors it was fighting, abuse, and addictions.   After a year of that somehow I got him to move us to Jonesboro to be closer to my family and I wanted to be at home.   I did all the arrangements of getting us there and even though D. was unhappy, I was happy.   I thought I had given up life at home to move to small McGehee so it was his turn.   Major mistake.

As we moved to Jonesboro I had plenty of help from my parents which began to allow me to have free time on my hands.   I didn't have to work because of D.'s good income so I had free time and money.   Root of all evil! I began to contact old friends because, of course, I needed a pill hook up.   I found it very easily and my addiction continued.   One day my world collided.   I ran into that boyfriend I had in high school (the bad one) and was in desperate need of pain pills.   Well, that he didn't have but he did have the devil heroin.   I couldn't find anything so I gave in and bought some and went somewhere I swore I'd never go.   He convinced me the only way to do it was to shoot it with a needle so at my desperate moment, I gave in and allowed him to give me a shot of it.   I fell in love.   It made me feel every way I wanted and I was on top of the world.   I felt powerful and care free.

I hid it for a very long time but when the heroin intake became as much as I did, I couldn't hide that amount of money each day from our account.   I began to lie to my parents telling them I had got a job and needed them to watch the baby while I worked.   It worked a few months.   I'd get dressed like I was going to work, take my son to my mom and meet up with whoever needed to make a run that day, collect due money and drive to Memphis for the pick up which I supplied my habit with as pay.   I'd make three or four trips a day if needed.   I was invincible I thought.   I won't get caught or anyone won't hurt me.   All along I was killing myself.

The addiction to the needle completely consumed my life.   I had been so angry, disgusted, disappointed and ashamed, until I had no feeling left.   I felt like all my morals as a human being were slowly fading away.   I was doing things to myself and to my husband and child behind their back, I pray now I never remember. One afternoon the life I had shattered.   I was ready to end my life.   I had jabbed a needle into my arms over fifty times trying to hit a vein for one last ultimate high that I had prayed would take me out and along with that I had developed a sickness of cutting myself so I could feel something and I hurt myself because I was angry that I had got this way.   How did I let *myself get this far?   One thing I know is that was all a work of the enemy and I had fell for it.   That day I had come to the end of my rope when my mom came in the bathroom.   I had over fifty holes and cuts up and down my arms dripping blood.   I looked up and said, "I need help."*

That day I'll never forget the way my mom looked crushed and so heart broke and disappointed. Luckily, my son was at his other nanna's and D. was at work, but what an issue to come home to.   I was carried to St. Bernard's and put on suicide watch as they proceeded to find help.   The next day D. came home and they carried me to Twin Rivers Hospital in Kennett, Missouri to the third floor to detox off heroin and counseling for the suicide.   It was literally a crazy house.   The people I lived with those five days had literally lost their minds and to this day I realize the reason God placed me in there alive was to show me how my life would be if I didn't stop what I was doing.

I felt better after detox and was ready to go home back to my husband and little son but boy was I wrong.   While I was there, D. had packed up our entire house and our son and moved back to McGehee. I came home to nothing.   It was one of the saddest days of my life.   I thought he would be there to help me get better and move forward but he either couldn't take it or didn't want to.   I won't ever know the reason why really, but honestly I don't blame him.   I couldn't even stand myself.   I was the most heartbroken I had ever been but the thing that hurt me the most was I hurt those two men in my life and everyone else around me.   So, along with my parents, we came to an agreement that long term help was the solution to get back my life with Jesus in it and my family back.   My brother, who was my best friend in the whole world, who had partied with me and ended up in trouble before I had, was finishing up a commitment at Mission Teens in Brazil, Indiana and had been trying to get my parents to get me help and had continually been praying for me.   I began to listen because I loved my brother and trusted him with all my heart.   He's my other rock to this day.   He always had hope in me and I saw a change in him and it was Jesus.   That's what I wanted.

I got accepted into Crossville, TN Mission Bible Training Center in 2011.   My brother and my dad drove me eight hours.   Those eight hours in the car with them were some of the best memories I had had in a long time.   There was hope in the car that day. Something I had lost.   I began a new life that day and will never forget it.   I continued in the program for seven months but one day I let the enemy sneak into my head and tell me I could go home.   Disguised as the voice from the Lord, I began to believe I was ready. As the enemy entered, I was not prepared.   I began to act weirdly and they decided I needed to add a few months more and I wasn't having it.   So I walked out of the Lord's will and was destined for disaster.   My family had been restored, I thought, and I was ready to come home to be the Proverbs 31 wife and mother. Little did I know I walked straight out into a trap.

The entire time I believed my husband was waiting, wanting his little family to work, he had been dating another girl who had been taking care of my son. When I left I was told he and the baby had got us a new house in Benton, Arkansas.   We knew no one there.   And yes, I came home to a beautiful new home, brand new car, and my little family in a new town.   New start, right?   So I thought.   All that stuff wasn't meant for me.   Just so happened he broke up with this other girl the night I called to tell him I was coming home and made it all look like the set up was for me, him and our son.   I found out about a week later and I relapsed.   I ended up taking some pain pills from my new neighbor who also told me when she met D. and our son he had told her I died and then proceeded to sleep with her too.   My world crushed again!   How could I have been so blind.   I guess I just wanted so badly to have a normal family and thought he would do right since I had been doing right.   I was a fool and should have known.   Like I had been taught, we were no longer equally yoked and down I went.

We fell fast and like it says it was seventy times worse. This time my son was older now and it took a lot to keep up and I began a new habit, meth.   D. still worked off and I would travel to his mom's or mine when he was gone and began smoking dope behind his back and everyone else's.   We eventually moved back to McGehee and I tried to rebuild clients for hair but one day when D. was home I was introduced to a past best friend of his who gave me more attention than my own husband.   He owned a farm and sold the best pot and dope around.   As D. left to go to work, this time J. came around.   I would hold amounts for him and took what I needed.   Before I knew it we had began an affair and I started working for him on pick ups and delivery.   I didn't want for anything.   I met people I should have never met and saw things I should not have seen.   I was running with some very wicked people that only thought of money and what they would get and didn't care who they hurt. Unfortunately, I picked up that mentality plus a million secrets only I can talk to God about for my own life's sake.   D. received a phone call of how I was living while he was away and came home in a rage, threatening me and I surrendered to him-once again trying to make it work.   But it just wouldn't.

We continued to argue and try to get back at one another and finally his mother took our son from us because honestly, he was the one getting hurt the most.   I decided to leave again and move home with my parents to try and start over again.   I continued in my mess hurting everyone in my way.   I had lost everything, my son, husband, career, reputation and most importantly, my relationship with God.   I ended up back with D. and our son in McGehee one last time and really tried but I couldn't quit the drugs.   I let the enemy tell me that they would be better off if I just went away.   So I did.   One night I left while they were asleep and moved to Shreveport, Louisiana with a man I had fell for in the drug game.   I wanted to escape from reality and I thought I would never have a normal life and was always going to be an addict.   I left everything I knew and ran off with the works of the devil.   The man I left with today lives for the Lord and went through the exact same thing I did, found the Lord again in jail and went to faith based treatment.   Funny how the Lord takes the things we do and did and turns it into something glorious for Him.

I lived though in Shreveport for five months and ended up homeless, hungry, miserable and lost everything. I made it back to Arkansas on my thirtieth birthday and to signing a set of divorce papers and losing custody of my son.   I really gave up when I faced all of that and ran straight towards the grave.   Anything I could inject I did, smoke I did, or take I did.   I had no hope and lost all sense of caring.   I finally decided on July 7th to surrender my life again to the Lord.   My brother who had been there through all my mess was in a mission serving the Lord and had been praying for twenty-seven weeks for me to give up and let the Lord take control of my life again.   I knew the whole time I needed to be back in Mission Teens.   I knew I could call the Mission throughout my mess.   It was my place of refuge.

On the 11th of July 2016, I gave up the battle to the One who wanted to fight for me the whole time.   I came into God's New Life ready and willing to let Jesus Christ have full control of my life and teach me His ways.   I was ready to transform, not conform, to His way of life.   These past seven months the Lord has truly set me down and literally worked a miracle in my life.   I came in with no hope or restoration but God.   He has given me a second chance at being a mother, daughter, sister and child of His.   I would not change a thing if this is what it had to take to get this relationship with Christ.   It all was worth it and I will continue to walk and serve the God that brought me through.   God bless, stay encouraged!

*

This young lady had it all didn't she?   But rejection was her demon.   Don't we all know what she felt? We have all been rejected.   The hurt from that sticks with a person, especially when you have felt it from a very young age into adulthood.   Satan knew just how to soothe that pain too, didn't he?   He was right there johnny-on-the-spot with the cure.

A life of privilege, personal success, and relationships down the tubes all for the love of some substance you can hold in your hand.   I am by no means attempting to patronize this young woman. She has thought the same thing many times-how could I have done all of that?

Drug abuse escalates until all at once you realize you are hooked.   Like the frog in the boiling water.   It starts out slow and easy going, a little pot smoking, then maybe a pill or two.   An emotional crisis comes along and you need something a little stronger to get you through it.   That little bit of something soon becomes not enough until it is *never* enough.   Then you find yourself in extremely hot water and you realize how dangerous a situation you are now in.

Drugs made this woman do things she would have never thought of doing just a few years earlier.   It caused conflict in every area of her life.   She compromised her Christian upbringing and values and when you do that, nothing will be right.   God said, "You are either for me or against me".   And God will not back up from that.   He doesn't allow a middle ground.   As my mother told us kids growing up when we would constantly slam the screen door running in and out of the house, "Stop slamming that door! You kids either get in or out. "

K.S. based her happiness on material things and other people.   Pretty clothes, money, a nice home and new cars-yes, those things are great but should not be our complete happiness.   Trying to please others, the constant dog and pony show, is setting yourself up for emotional failure.   And that is easy to do when you are a mother and wife.   Aren't we women taught self sacrifice for the sake of the children, home, and husband?   It is considered selfish if we take time for ourselves or something other than caring for the family.   However, true inner happiness can only come from God.   That peace and joy that walking your life with God can bring cannot be outdone by anything or anyone on Earth.   Yes, love your husband, love your children, care for your home and acquire things that make you happy.   God means for us to be happy.   But your soul should long for, thirst for, should have great desire to commune with your heavenly Father, the number one love of your life.   He holds the greatest love of all, the greatest happiness that can be experienced.   Happiness through God is the only way to live.

This woman turned to many things but not God in an effort to drown her hurts.   If she had taken her cares to Him at the start, He could have comforted her and kept her strong so as to resist the temptations spread in front of her.   She sees that now.   She is strong now.   She is willing to do what God the Father demands of her because she has learned He is the only answer to her problems, to her aching heart.   God will not compromise as she once did.   She knows now He is the key to true happiness.

Let's keep K.S. in our prayers that she will remain in God's will and that God will restore a relationship with her family.

LIFE STORY #3

Female, 36 years of age

I was born in Kansas City, Missouri, July 25th, 1980, to two people who loved me very much.   My dad was a Baptist minister and my mom played piano and taught Sunday School.   When I was two years old I was molested by a man that was not my father.   I'm not sure exactly how many times this happened but one is too many.   My parents ended up divorcing in 1983.   My dad took me one day because back then whoever had the child got custody.   He tried to salvage their marriage and gave me back to my mom.

But the damage was already done so with the divorce final, me and my mom moved to St. Louis, Missouri. Just me and her in a two bedroom house. I loved it.   I remember dancing with my mom in the living room to oldies music.   I remember being six years old and I picked up a beer bottle on the side of the road to throw and it cut me and I ran to the neighbor's house because my mom was at work and I had to go to the hospital and get stitches.   I always hung out with the wrong type of people and did things I wasn't supposed to do.

My mom met my step-dad and he was really good to me and my mom yet I still missed my real dad.   I remember going to see him and riding on a plane all by myself.   I must have been six and I got off the plane and he was standing there with a new wife and her four kids.   After that, I only remember a handful of times that I saw my dad.   I remember sitting on the front steps, bags packed and arguing with my mom that Dad was going to come and pick me up-that this time he would show up.   He never did.   So I felt like I wasn't good enough and I started to look for attention in the wrong places.

My first sexual experience was when I was ten years old with someone who lived up the street from me and who was the same sex as me.   When I was twelve I started smoking cigarettes and hanging around people that were eighteen, nineteen because I thought it was cool.   When I was twelve I started taking vicodin and drinking out of my mom and step-dad's liquor cabinet.   They never noticed.   I sneaked out almost every night, started skipping school and met this guy who was twenty-two.   I thought I was special.   I mean he told me I was pretty and more mature and so I let him do things I shouldn't have and never told anyone.   I never saw him again.

After that, I just didn't care anymore.   And my drinking and mixing pills got worse.   When I was fourteen, I started tripping acid and tried heroin for the first time and it was like Heaven.   All my problems disappeared and I felt like I was floating on a cloud.   I met this boy halfway through my freshman year.   He was on the soccer team and told me I was too nice to be putting stuff like drugs in my body, that weed and drinking were okay.   So I quit.   I remember him telling me that I was meant for more. We were friends and nothing more.   I can still remember the day I got the news that he died.   My sophomore year in April.   Him and his younger brother were in a car accident.   And both of them died.   I found out over the PA system in first hour Math class.   At the viewing all of us were high but I remember seeing his mom and she was upset and crying but still put together.   She had four other boys and I was thinking, 'I wonder how she's not lost it'.   I wish I had that.   That was God.   Only I didn't know it then.

My mom thought I was losing it.   I rarely stayed at home.   Drank a lot, started doing cocaine and using older men to get whatever I wanted.   I graduated at seventeen.   How, I am not really sure.   I didn't really hang out with kids my age and didn't want to go on a senior trip with them.   So the school offered an educational tour, seven countries in fourteen days. My parents thought it might be what I needed, a break from the people I was around and a good opportunity. So I saved up half and they paid the rest.   I don't remember much of it because I was drunk the whole time but I have pictures and when I look at them I can halfway remember some things.   When I got back things went kind of back to normal.   (FOOTNOTE: I met this guy and thought I had found it.   Lost my daughter and quit caring about anything) I started hanging out in pool halls and met C. who was a cocaine and weed dealer.   I went from living at home to living with him in a month.   I remember thinking it was so cool having my own house and in love or so I thought.

The first time he hit me was at his parent's house and his dad said, "If you gonna' hit her, fine, but at least take her outside first." I didn't know what to say. This went on for almost a year.   So I started doing more cocaine and drinking.   My best friend was a stripper so I'd sell to her and her friends.   One day she convinced me to get on stage with her and I saw how much money it made and I was hooked.   I remember going from one-hundred fifty pounds to one-hundred and five pounds because being one-hundred and ten was fat leave (meaning I was too fat to work) so I started throwing up after I ate so I wouldn't gain any more weight.   I went home one day and remember my mom saying, "Oh, honey, you look like you have a cold, your nose is so red and raw. Let me get you some cream."   So I left and thought how can I do this and not be noticed?

So C. bought me a needle.   My life spiraled out of control after that.   I tried meth and would mix the two.   I don't remember a large part of what went on until I was twenty-one and me and C. got into a fight and he banged my head into the fridge and tried to kill me.   Luckily, someone came by and threatened to call the police.   I left and never looked back, stayed at my mom's for a couple of months but she had rules and that just wasn't happening so I moved in with a girl I knew since high school and things were crazy.   I lived to get high and started hanging out around people who cooked meth.   All my days started blending together to where weeks felt like one long day.

One night my parents went out and me and my so-called friends went to their house and started drinking.   There was something in my drink and after the first one, I don't remember anything until I woke up the next morning.   My mom called my phone and said, "The house was robbed."   So I went to their (my friend's) house and got most all of my parent's stuff back.   I couldn't get a camera that had film of my grandpa who had died still in it.   My parents took my key, changed the locks, and told me they were through.

So I made money anyway I could and started staying on people's couches or motel rooms.   That's where I met D., my son's dad.   He sold meth and I started hanging out with him and people that cooked dope every other day.   I called home one day and found out that my step-dad had a heart attack. Too much stress for me and I asked for a needle and it went downhill from there.   I started stealing anhydrous for the meth because of the rush I got.   And went and sold it with D.   He took me to a house and I met my best friend there and D. would do his thing and me and her would go party.   On St. Patrick's Day, I got my first DWI.   I spent twenty-fours hours in jail with them asking me all kinds of questions for an hour or two about if I knew this person or that one.   I knew then I was being watched but still didn't care.   I just got more aware of my surroundings.

Me and D. eventually got caught and arrested for intent to attempt to manufacture and possession of pseudo ephedrine.   I slept for three days and then kept getting sick so they gave me a pregnancy test and yes, I was pregnant.   Two weeks later, my parents got me out and I went to rehab where they told me I had an addiction to money not drugs and let me out fifteen days later because my insurance ran out.   My parents co-signed me and D. an apartment and things were great.   I quit drugs until one day D. slid me a foil and said if I didn't smoke it he was leaving.   I was six months pregnant and figured one time wouldn't hurt. One time turned into every once in a while and then every day.   Then he left me with all the bills due, pregnant and nothing to do.   I remember going to my baby shower high as a kite.

My son was born, six pounds, thirteen ounces and healthy.   But since I had tested positive at a doctor's visit they sent Nurses for Newborns to my house which was okay with me.   My mom would get up with the baby because I just couldn't bond with him.   I wouldn't allow myself to love him the right way and felt like he was better off without me.   I tried but depression took over me and fear of losing him messed with me so I did what I always did, moved back to my apartment and got high to kill the pain.   Me and T., a good friend of mine, started dating and he moved in with me.   When my son was ten months old, I got busted again and found out T. set me up to take the fall.   I was also pregnant again.   This time, I was done with the drugs and was going to try to do things right.   I had toxemia and preclampsia during my pregnancy and was hospitalized when I was seven and a half months pregnant.   I started getting sick and the doctor's told me there was something wrong. My worst fear. I felt like I was being punished. The baby had tied a knot in the cord and wrapped it around his neck and they had to send me into immediate labor to undue the cord from his neck or he wouldn't make it.

He was born June 25th, four pounds, six ounces and had to stay in the hospital for ten days but was perfectly healthy. They were the longest ten days of my life. I went to see him every day and prayed to God I would change if He would just let my son be okay. On August 19th, I went to prison and did one-hundred twenty days treatment and five years paper (probation). After my one-hundred twenty, I got out and tried to do right. I went to drug classes at the parole office and D., my first son's dad was there and offered me a ride home and had some drugs so it was on again. I couldn't say no. He's doing life in prison now for drugs. I tried to do right and moved to the city and got a job and did good for about a year then fell off again and lost my apartment, so I went back to live with mom and my boys.

I still had my job and got clean for a couple of months then one day at a friend's, she pulled out some heroin. I just wanted to escape from life for awhile. At twenty-seven, I was addicted so badly I couldn't keep a job, stole from my kid's piggy bank to get high, did anything so I wouldn't be sick. I wouldn't stop. I watched six friends die of overdoses in a three month period because it was cut with fentanyl. I went to the parole office and begged to go to prison because I was scared I was going to die.   He said he just couldn't send me to prison.   I had no violations.   So one month later I had fifteen and got my wish.   I bounced from jail to jail and they put me on methadone to come off the heroin.   Then I had to detox off it.

I went to prison for two years, one month and fifteen days.   I had lost any hope that my life would ever be anything good.   My real dad wrote me and told me I could parole to Rector, Arkansas if I went to a faith-based program.   And I figured what do I have to lose? Nobody else wanted me around.   So I went.   On July 4th, I found out T. died.   He jumped off a bridge.   I didn't deal with it-just stuffed it down and moved on. T. was my youngest son's dad.   Three months into a four month faith-based program, all women, I met my husband.   He came there to see his mom.   In August, I saw him again and I finished my four months and he was there to pick me up.   On August 21st, we were married and on October 30th, we were arrested with two Class Y felonies for manufacturing. On December 21st, I went to court and because of my previous record they offered me one-hundred thirty-six months. My husband went in there and took the charges and signed on ten years if they would drop my charges so they did.   I went back expecting to go to a Missouri prison for a parole violation and got told they re-filed my charges so I went to court in January and they offered me six months county, long-term rehab, and one-hundred thirty-six months suspended imposition of sentence because the judge said there was no way that I didn't know what was going on.

So I did my six months and went to the same rehab and graduated. I got a good job and stayed with a friend. I met a guy at Celebrate Recovery and we started dating. I told my husband that I wanted a divorce and me and K. moved in together. Seven months later I got papers that my parents wanted to adopt my boys and I had a miscarriage and was sent home from work. I didn't even know I was pregnant. Rather than dealing with any of this I went and got high. Morphine and pain pills to dull the pain. This went on for another ten months until I left K. for him stealing from a friend of mine and called my husband for money. He came to see me and didn't recognize me. I had lost almost 80 lbs. He told me to get in the car and he wasn't taking no for an answer. I told him we'd go tomorrow and we talked and I begged him for forgiveness. The next day we went to MJ's and I detoxed for almost two weeks and me and my husband moved into our own place. We did good for a while but his brother came over one day and we weren't strong enough to say no, so here we go again. We let some people move in with us to pay the rent and that didn't work out so we stayed from place to place and ended up at a homeless shelter. Too hard to do drugs there so we moved in with some people where we could do what we wanted. Did whatever we had to do to get by until he went to jail and I went back to the homeless shelter. This kept up for awhile and I just got sick of it. We moved in with his aunt when he got out.

Different town, different people, running from parole, we got in a bad motorcycle accident and I told him to run because I dislocated my knee and I couldn't.   This way one of us was free.   Looking back now, I don't know what I was thinking.   I had two black eyes, cuts all over my face and a dislocated knee.   So off to jail I go.   I was so messed up that no one recognized me until I spoke.   There was eight of us in there that all hung out together and we all went to prison.   I prayed before court that I'd do the right thing and quit running from God if He'd make a miracle happen and I didn't get my S.I.S. Well, He made a miracle.

Four years was what they offered and I signed before they could change their minds.   I got to prison May 25th and went to a program called P.A.L.S. (religious-Principles and Applications for Life Situations) on June 4th.   I found hope in a very hopeless situation and began to learn about God and gain a personal relationship.   I vowed not to let my time be a waste and to do something with it.   So I took a couple college classes and then took therapeutic community because the board strongly suggested it.   I did two years to the day and went to a halfway house in Little Rock, did meetings, got a sponsor and a job at Sonic. I did good for five months then I went and stayed the day with my husband and that is where my life got worse than it had ever been.

I was so tormented and hopeless.   My husband took someone's vehicle and left me with them and they held me as collateral and told me they were going to handcuff me and put me in a storage shed. Everything went crazy after that.   I quit using and pleaded with the Lord.   All I wanted was to die and end my suffering.   I felt like I ruined everything I touched.   The Lord stepped in and I got arrested. My dad came to see me and said, "There is a place called Mission Teens and you need to go to it".   My mom said she was done.   I would not see the boys again.   I had no one and nothing.   My husband was doing God knows what and I had given up.   I did ninety days split up in county jail and in prison.   Yes, back again.   A lady next to me told me she didn't want to see me but at least I made it back.   So many don't.   She didn't want me to spend my life in prison and told me God had greater plans.   So I paroled out to my aunt who I never knew and decided to go to God's New Life.   Only problem was I couldn't take my depression and anxiety medicine and no bed was available for three weeks.   The people there were so nice, gave me numbers to call them anytime and prayed with me, gave me scriptures and I looked at them and wanted what they had-peace and joy and a sense that things were going to be okay.   I was so broken that when I came for a devotion and the girls prayed with me I had to stop in the middle and take a moment.   These strangers that were telling me they were praying for me and they loved me.   I'd never had that.   People that never met me yet cared so much.   I knew I was home.

So I went off my meds, came here three weeks later and it's been a rough road.   Looking at yourself and the things you have done isn't easy but it's the best thing I've ever done.   This place has saved my life.   I have graduated and decided to stay on for staff training.   I want to give back to the place that gave *me hope for a future, knowledge of the word of God and a peace that I never thought possible.   I stayed because I wanted my life to bring glory to God and if I could be used to help someone not have to go through all the pain and heartache I did, it would be worth it.*

The devil had a plan for my life to steal, kill and destroy me but Jesus came to give me life and life more abundantly and that is what He has done.   And I know this is just the beginning.   All I have to do is put God first and seek His will for my life.   I have something I've never had before, to be content no matter what my circumstances are.   Now when things come my way I take them to the Lord.   I have a relationship with my family again and for the first time I talk to my kids and they want to talk to me. The Lord has done more than I could have ever imagined and I can't wait to see what He does next.

*

What a life this woman has had!   I don't see how she has survived.   The lack of acceptance, an apparent abuse perpetrated upon her as a toddler, love withheld and the feeling of being unwanted began early in her life.   Her parent's divorce and her father's subsequent remarriage with new children, leaving her behind, was very hurtful to her as a child.

Parents just don't realize the harm that a divorce causes their children.   Their whole world structure crashes when a parent leaves the home.   In abuse situations of course, their lives may become much better.   That is, if the remaining parent doesn't take on the pattern of jumping into another abusive relationship, and dragging the children into it as well.

When a child loves a parent and that parent leaves the home due to divorce, the child many times becomes withdrawn, reclusive, and looks for something to fill the void.   Read this excerpt from an article from "Focus on the Family", How Could Divorce Affect My Kids?, by Amy Desai, J.D. ---

Research comparing children of divorced parents to children with married parents shows:

Children from divorced homes suffer academically. They experience high levels of behavioral problems. Their grades suffer, and they are less likely to graduate from high school.

Kids whose parents divorce are substantially more likely to be incarcerated for committing a crime as a juvenile.

Because the custodial parent's income drops substantially after a divorce, children in divorced homes are almost five times more likely to live in poverty than are children with married parents.

Teens from divorced homes are much more likely to engage in drug and alcohol use, as well as sexual intercourse than are those from intact families.

Before you say, "Not my kid," remember that the children and teens represented in these statistics are normal kids, probably not much different from yours. Their parents didn't think they would get involved in these things, either. Again, we're looking at increased risks.

A few more statistics to consider:

Children from divorced homes experience illness more frequently and recover from sickness more slowly.

They are also more likely to suffer child abuse.

Children of divorced parents suffer more frequently from symptoms of psychological distress.

And the emotional scars of divorce last into adulthood.

The scope of this last finding — children suffer emotionally from their parents' divorce — has been largely underestimated. Obviously, not every child of divorce commits crime or drops out of school. Some do well in school and even become high achievers. However, we now know that even these children experience deep and lasting emotional trauma.

For all children, their parents' divorce colors their view of the world and relationships for the rest of their lives.

Wallerstein Study---
Psychologist Judith Wallerstein followed a group of children of divorce from the 1970's into the 1990's. Interviewing them at 18 months and then 5, 10, 15 and 25 years after the divorce, she expected to find that they had bounced back. But what she found was dismaying: Even 25 years after the divorce, these children continued to experience substantial expectations of failure, fear of loss, fear of change and fear of conflict.(*end of article excerpt*)

So, we see that divorce is extremely harsh on children.   From the way our young lady's story goes, her life went downhill after her parents divorced.   When she was old enough to start feeling the real emotional impact, the missing father figure, she looked for something to fill the void, the puzzle piece that could never truly be found so she found solace in escape. Escape from life, responsibilities and emotional let-downs and into a drug fueled world where there were no demands made on her.

I know S.P. is in a better place now and is getting the kind of soul nourishing help she needs to get past the hard life she has had.   God can and will do a miracle for her and she has taken that step of faith toward Him to make the miracle of a new life for herself happen.

LIFE STORY #4

Male, 44 years of age

My name is B.D.B.   It hasn't always been that, so let me tell you my story.   My mother is from Granite City, Illinois a small town across the Mississippi River from St. Louis, Missouri.   When she turned eighteen in 1970, her goal was to get away from a very controlling father.   She got a job at Bussman Fuse in St. Louis and got an apartment.   My father's family owned a bar and this is where my mom met him.   My father's family were a real rough crowd.   Well, the boys anyway.   My father had already served prison time and was involved in prostitution and running girls of the night.   Who knows but God what my mom saw in him or how she put up with that mess. Anyhow, September 18th, 1972, I was born in Barnes-Jewish Hospital in St. Louis.   I was given the name J.D.M. JR.   So this is all I know is that my father had used a pistol and hit my mom in the head and she had him put in prison.   And during that time my mom changed my name to B.

Now really my first memory starts about the age of four.   My mom and dad were getting back together. My momma and I were moving to Bakersfield, California.   My father had gotten out of prison there and had established himself.   Being a young boy I didn't understand that he was a convict.   All I knew was he was my dad and like any young boy I wanted to be like him.   I dressed like him and went everywhere with him and my mom was made to stay home.   I can recall we had a lot of fighting chickens and my father and I would go to illegal fights.   I had no idea that we were doing anything wrong at first. He taught me to fight with his friends.   Really he was one to carry a pistol and not scared to use it.   I didn't realize that everything I was being taught by him was bad.   Mostly I was only around his friends and their kids.   So it was all just normal for me.   I got my first realization one day when I was at work with him at old man W.'s shoe repair.   He was smoking a pipe and not knowing, I asked him what he was smoking in it.   And he told me cherry tobacco and I told him that I smoked pot in mine.   What took place after that made me realize that was bad.   He was furious and went off on my dad.   My mom looked very scared. And up to this point in my life I had seen him beat my mom many times and I realized that was going to happen to me, too.   And I had all day to see the look on his face that told me so.   That night was something that changed the way I thought about him forever.   On the ride home he told me how I was never supposed to tell anything we did at home or anywhere.   My mom was begging him to not do anything, that I didn't know I said something wrong. This turned out to be the longest night of my life at about five years old.   He beat me with a belt and with his fist.   My mom tried to stop him and the way that he beat her was tragic.   And when I tried to help he picked me up and threw me through a wall.   I could not breathe at all for what seemed like forever.

Finally, when I could breathe, I saw he had a rope around my mom's neck and strung her up in the living room standing in a chair, pistol out.   I was very scared.   He had his friend come get me and I stayed with them overnight.   I didn't know if I would ever see her alive again.

Thank God the next day when my dad came and got me he was nice to me and told me to never tell what had happened and he loved me.   From there on I knew he was a liar and one day I would be big enough to fight back.   And when I seen my mom looking like Rockie after he had lost a fight, I really wanted to learn everything I could about fighting so I could protect us.

For awhile, I spent a lot of time with my mom while my dad was at work.   He didn't take us with him anymore.   She taught me how to read and write. Preparing me for school.   There was a lot more of this explosive rage out of my father beating us. Smoking pot with him afterwards helped me to block it all out.   Not to mention my mom would tell me to do whatever he said and don't help her.   She could take care of whatever he did to her.

I was looking forward to going to school because I just wanted to get away.   The problem of starting school was I didn't know how to be a kid and I was held back in kindergarten.   There was a lot of struggle of being too scared to tell what was going on at home because teachers would ask and I would not tell out of fear. My father opened his own shoe repair and for awhile we lived in the back of the shop.   The craziness never stopped.   My dad had, what I thought, gone crazy and pulled out his pistol and started shooting it and a bullet ricocheted and landed in front of me.   And he told me to pick it up.   It was hot and as I was shaking it in my hand he told me to hold it tight cause the next one to come out of the gun was going through me.   I just stood there for what seemed like forever.   The neighbor came over and asked if I could come over and have cake and ice cream for his grandaughter's birthday and I went.   My mom was over there and we left with some of my dad's friends.

My dad almost died of spinal meningitis.   So for the next few months because he was hospitalized my mom and I ran the shop.   And she promised we would leave although we never did.   He got out of the hospital and it wasn't long and all this craziness came back. My little brother was born and we moved into a house in Lamont, California on Weedpatch Highway.

I never stopped trying to help my mom when he would beat her.   And so my bus driver would always talk to me because it was just between her and myself for most of the ride.   I wore a lot of long sleeve shirts and turtlenecks and she would ask me why and I would lie and say I liked them.   The end of all this was right around the corner.

My other little brother was born six months before my eighth birthday.   My mom had just about died having him.   My dad had took me to the hospital with him and pulled a gun on the doctor, put it to his head and told him that if she died so would he.   He dragged me out of the hospital shooting the gun telling people to get out of the way.   There was a high speed chase and we made it to some friends' house.   Then he threw me out of the car and they got me before the police caught up with us.   There was a bunch of them and for the first time I got to see him get his from the officers.

I have always wondered how he got out of jail so fast but he did and it wasn't that long and it started again. The first time I ran away my friend's mom found me in their barn and took me home.   My mom promised again that we would get away just give her some time to work it out.   My dad promised not to hit me no more.

The next time he did, I went and stole a bicycle and rode it into town.   As it got dark the arcade that I was at noticed that I was too young to be by myself and they called the police.   They did listen when I told them about what was going on but they took me home.   My father was so mad that he beat me like never before.   He tied me to one of the palm trees and put a sprinkler on me all night.   When morning came, he turned it off and told me to get dressed for school. I did-long sleeves and a turtleneck to hide the bruises. I got on the bus and the bus driver started in with it. "Gonna' be hot", that I should go get a T-shirt and shorts and she would wait.   I never forgot the sadness she had on her face when I told her I can't.   It was the last day of school.   The pressure I felt with every teacher asking me why I would wear that on such a hot day and I could talk to them.   They wanted to help me.   I just wanted the day to end so I could go home and run far away.   The bus driver lady talked to me on the way home when it was just us.   She even cried and told me she could help.

I decided I was gonna' take my dad's best fighting dog and chicken and some money and leave.   After I packed this stuff up, I went to the Mexican lady's house next door that rented from my dad.   When I told her I needed to go to Bakersfield, at first she said no, that my father is loco and has guns.   But when I lifted up my shirt and showed her she cried and changed her mind and took me to another lady's house, my babysitter before we moved because she hated my dad.   It did not turn out like I had planned.   She let me in but she said almost the same thing, I can't stay there that my dad is crazy and he will come there with his friends and guns.   So I told everything that had been going on.   She said she would find me some place to hide.   I was very shocked when the California Hiway Patrol pulled up and came to the door.   He asked me to pull up my shirt and I did.   Tears welled up in his eyes and he hugged me and told me this would never happen to me again.

I spent the rest of that day with him going to the hospital.   At first I didn't realize that with my body being eighty-five percent bruised that it was so serious until after every person I came into contact with that day cried, hugged me, and all were very mad.

I was taken to a place where they took children from

birth to eighteen waiting to go up to a foster home, adopted, or until the parents satisfied the courts and got their children back.   All the staff there were really nice to me at first until I started getting into a lot of fights with the other boys.   I was counseled a lot about how hitting others is not how to resolve my problems.   I really did not understand so it caused me to be isolated from the other kids.   Which was to me better because I spent my school time with a staff member doing my assignments.   And then helping with the smaller babies up to age four.   I guess because I had been taking care of my little brother I was used to it.

Slowly over time I started to be allowed to spend time in the ad wing with kids my age.   And for whatever reason I would be fighting again.   That was always what I got into trouble for.   Over the course of eight years old to just before my eleventh birthday, it was about two years before I even talked to or seen my mom and my brothers.   I was in four different foster homes.   The first one didn't want me anymore because I would fight back when they would spank me.   The second was just a temporary for a weekend. The third, I was molested and abused and taken from. The last was a good one and I stayed there until my mom got me back.   During that last foster home I had always went by J. or Little J.   They started calling me B., which did not work for me at all until I had a visit with my mom and she explained that she had changed my name back when I was just a few months old.   I didn't like B. D. B. but needless to say I got used to it.   So my mom got me back and because of what we both had been through, I think she felt guilty and pretty much let me do what I wanted to.   I started the new school and that's never easy at first.   I was in trouble at school for fighting but I ended up getting a lot of friends because I was not a pushover.

Things settled down after the new wore off.   I started hanging around older kids and their older brothers. I started smoking cigs and pot.   Gangs were mostly black and mexican kids.   Although I had a lot of run-ins with these groups,   I would always try to talk them out of wanting to fight 'cause I really didn't want to fight and that's what it always came down to.   And for whatever reason they quit bothering me after I had fought the kid G. M.   I had gained his respect and made it clear I would not be joining any gang even if I had to fight every one of them.   And with the white kids, there was a group of us who were just friends, pot heads, stoners, metal heads.   At least that's what the other groups labeled us.

I had been questioned by the police about a couple of purse thefts and later on in the summer about two racing bicycles before I was to start eighth grade.   A lot of my friends for one reason or another were in juvenile detention.   A couple had been shot and killed or stabbed to death by gang members.   I was charged with two counts of theft and two counts of grand theft at age thirteen.   I was looking at being sent to youth authorities in Los Angeles, California. But my judge was also the same judge over my case when my dad was sent to prison for what he had done to me.   He dropped the felonies to misdemeanors and

I was given four years probation, community service and some theft classes.

I was getting high, drinking and at this time, I had tried just about every drug there is but I just stuck with drinking and pot.   Who really knows how I did well in school but I always did even though I was stoned most of the time.   I was given an allotted time to do the community service and theft classes but I never did them.   I graduated eighth grade, summer came and I received violation papers and a court date. My mom and step-dad Larry really didn't know how to reach me so mom had gotten hold of probation and they said I was going to be taken into custody and sent to YA for the remainder of my probation.   So my mom asked if she moved me back east to St. Louis if they would come get me, but it turned out because it was only a misdemeanor probation, I just wouldn't be able to come back to California until after my eighteenth birthday.   So they decided to move me to Granite City, Illinois.   Before we left Bakersfield, CA my mom took me and my little brothers to see my father.   My brothers stayed the weekend with him but I was not because I didn't trust him after everything that had happened and I really thought my momma was crazy for allowing my brothers to.   So we moved and it was a month before my fifteenth birthday.

I had never known any family up to this point in my life.   And I didn't fit in well with my long hair and heavy metal style especially in a hick town.   Granite City is one.   My mom's friends tried to act like everything was perfect and they loved me.   We were family.   I didn't have any problem letting them know they were liars.   If they were family they would have been there for us when we needed them.   To me they were fake and acted like nothing ever happened.   I started high school, ninth grade.   I have a cousin who is just a couple of months younger than me so I made friends fast.   Also because I talked different and looked different it was alright with the girls but with the guys my age well, I will just say my first day of school I was in trouble for fighting.   I really didn't want to fight anymore and in 1987, it would turn out to be pretty much the end of it.   I got the label, 'Don't mess with him, he's crazy', with the guys in school. It's funny to me looking back 'cause I got the nickname 'California Kid, please don't make me fight'. So after the new wore off, I smoked pot and drank every day.   My step-dad stayed in California although a year later he decided to show up.   My real father on the other hand died of an overdose January, 1987, five months after we moved to Granite City.   Seeing how I was his oldest son I had to sign the release papers at a notary to get his body sent to Kennett, MO where his family is from so I got to meet them.   They told me they had tried to get me when I was in foster care and I do remember asking my case worker what their last name was and he said M. and I told them I wasn't going with anyone from his family.   I felt bad because they were really nice people.   I never stayed in touch after the funeral.

I got a job the summer before my sixteenth birthday and met a girl who I was with for close to three years.

I really lived at her house and my friends more than at my mom's 'cause I had got caught with pot and my step-dad was always on me about it.   So my girlfriend had gotten pregnant and although I didn't know at the time she went to her aunt's for a month. But at the end of 1990 she came back telling me she had an abortion and that ended that.

I was coming up on my senior year of high school working selling pot by the pounds and selling guns on occassion.   I was doing most of this at strip clubs and ended up getting a place with two of the girls from the club.   One had a son six months old and the other girl's husband had just killed himself.   I only had a half hour study hall class and a two and half hour VOC auto shop class until January of 1991 ended and then I would graduate-all the while hustling pot and working as a shift leader all before turning eighteen. Life got real crazy when one of the girls' cousin got out of prison.   I got kicked out of school for missing too many days while being in the CO-OP program. The cousin was only out of prison a week and started doing commercial burglaries again and he asked if I would let him use my car for the night for five-hundred dollars up front and five-hundred dollars after the job was done and he would rent me a motel room, supply whatever I wanted, and a couple of girls. For an eighteen year old boy it seemed like the only thing to do.   Every night after that really became a blur and it lasted about two months and my car got left behind when they had to run.   So when they made it back, I got real drunk and went to the police department and reported it stolen just to cover myself.

McDonald's Burgers was laying off and my step-dad was being transferred to San Jose, CA and my mom told me if I wanted to go back to Bakersfield pop would put me to work and seeing how this current situation had got too hot it was a good idea.   I could get away.   So my first night back I called my step-dad and my uncle and they were having a long time no see party and since I was eighteen I was told that I could join in.   I didn't know and neither did they know that this would be the start of my love affair with meth.

My step-dad went to San Jose and I stayed with nana and pop and all my step-cousins.   I worked with pop remodeling houses making anywhere from seven-hundred to a thousand dollars a week and running with my old friends from junior high and grade school. Meth and parties became a weekend thing.   This lasted about a year.   Pop and I had a falling out.   So I ended up living with my uncle and aunt for a couple of months before I went and stayed with my aunt's brother.   He had owned a hot rod speed shop but had been in a bad accident and it was closed.   So he was still working on muscle cars and he realized I knew how to work on cars and he had a lot of Arab friends with hot rods that wanted them fixed.   He always had meth so that's what I woke up to most of the time.   I would be up three days at a time.

I was going to parties all the time, fighting with the gang bangers. The Rodney King riots broke out and one night coming home from a party I was jumped by two Mexican gang members.   One of them hit me in the face with a pipe which should have killed me considering it broke both sides of my jaw, my nose, and I had sixteen eye socket fractures.   How I fought them off and managed to get to the 7-11 around the corner, only God knows.   I didn't realize how bad I was hurt until my aunt's brother and my little cousin JJ came up after I had called and told them where I was.   JJ started crying as soon as he saw me.   The cops were asking me questions when I got up.   The lady officer grabbed me by my eye and my legs collapsed from the pain and the EMT's rushed through the door of the store, cut my shirt off and that's all I remember until I woke up in the hospital the next morning.   I had a softball-sized knot on the right side of my face.   That whole day was tests, being scanned, CAT scans.   They sewed up the cut with nothing but local anesthesia because of the eye socket fractures. I didn't realize how incoherent I was for about a month.

Reality set in and I realized I needed to get back to the midwest where my life expectancy was longer.   My parents let me stay with them in Granite City.   I got a job, a car and an apartment with their help.   I thought I was done with the meth and I would just smoke and sell pot.   I still had connections with the major pot dealers and the guys I used to supply were more than happy to have a steady connection.   So I was working for SHP.   I had decided to go see if R. N. had gotten out of prison.   When I went to his grandma's where he lived, a hot blonde answered the door and when I asked for him she was very disrespectful.   She said he was at J.'s and slammed the door.   I knocked again, she answered with a bad attitude and I calmly told her that she might treat R.'s friends like that but she was not going to treat me like that and that I had not been around for two years and where does J. live?   I didn't realize what would come of that but she showed me where he lived, so talk about good timing, when I knocked on J's door, it was like I never left.   They were counting their money to get a quarter pound of pot so we worked it all out.   I would come over every day to give them what they needed.   When I went out to my car to get my stuff here is this blonde with the bad attitude saying, "Hey sexy you".   Leaving, I nicely told her no.   She followed me back inside and R. told her to go back home for a few.   I found out it was his little sister and after everything had been done, she came back.   Her name was L. and she would become my wife and the mother of both my son and daughter.

So for about a year all was well working and selling pot, then meth showed up.   I knew I had to be careful messing with that stuff because my connections would cut me off the weed if they found out I was messing with the hard drugs.   So one Saturday morning, when I would go to get my supply, the guys, who were violent like my dad, told me that if they found out I was messing with that meth again, it would be over with.   It all came to a big halt when a big federal indictment came out and I lost my connection.   The town dried up, twenty-one people went to prison.

So I was thinking it's best I stopped before I lost my freedom.   Besides, my son was just born.   My *parents moved to Missouri and a month later, I would follow because the company I worked for was moving to Wentzville, Missouri.   So I switched departments going from mold repair to marble pouring and casting work, second shift.   My life was great being a husband and a father and spending weekends doing the family thing.   L. and I still smoked pot and got it from a guy at work every week.   So it didn't take time away from my family.   I stayed on the Missouri side of the river and not going to the Illinois side because I had several warrants for all different stuff from DUI to misdemeanor possession.*

One Friday night after work I had went to the bar and then to a guy's house I worked with.   I was drunk and decided I would sleep it off but at five a.m. when I woke up and left, my car heater quit working and it was twenty-eight degrees.   I was doing 65 in a 55 and got pulled over.   The officer noticed I was cold and asked why I was speeding.   I told him my heater was out and I was trying to get home so he told me to come get in his car to get warmed up while he wrote me some tickets.   And when he finished writing them he smelled alcohol on me so after the breath test I was legally drunk but he was still nice and let me call someone to get the car and take me home.   I got two years probation and did all the DWI stuff.

Other than this, life was all I had hoped for one day it would be.   I was offered a supervisor's position but I would have to switch to day shift and L. was going to have our second child, a little girl.   So here I was working days.   I got to know the guys on day shift which I kind of knew already because I would get to work an hour early.   D. lived close to me and we were on lunch one day and I rode with him to get something to eat.   I guess pot heads always get along because we were always looking for the best weed.   So I started getting more for both of us.   I met M. who had just started with the company and I was training him.   We had went to lunch and he had really good pot.   Needless to say, I started getting mine from him and it all got way past what I had planned and I was dealing again.   I did it all at work or to people who worked with my little brother.   I met a guy who wanted to trade meth for pot and in 1997, Missouri had a big meth problem and before long I had made a name for myself in this.

My daughter was born in August.   I was still just dealing at work but everywhere I went the police were sure to be close behind trying to catch me.   I was trying to buy some property and a house.   I had everything worked out with the finance company. The problem came because I ruptured a disc in my back and when I was able to go back to work my company wanted me to switch to a sprayer since the casting department was heavy work.   I told them to let me take a week vacation to see if I could find a different job and I got a UAW union job at BMP.   So switching jobs stopped the finance company from going forward.   Also, switching jobs turned out to be a bad choice because now selling drugs became a way of life.

I stopped doing family stuff.   I justified it to my wife

and parents by saying I had people's cars to fix which was true but I had selfish motives-to sell drugs and use.   Somewhere along the way I started shooting up and my wife had too.   I had gotten into manufacturing and the people I was doing it with started getting busted by the feds.   In the latter part of the summer of 1999 my life had become work during the week and manufacture on the weekend. L. was sick of it and told me she would not take me to where I needed to go so I called my friend's sister who had went to prison and she sent someone to get me.

That night it all went bad.   I recall just a few days before being fed up with it all and out loud asking God to take me away from it all and He did, just not the way I would have liked it.   That night I had left where I was doing this stuff and was pulled over and taken to jail for manufacturing meth along with a bunch of other stuff.   My bond was $100,000 cash only.   At the preliminary hearings a good lawyer got it to a ten percent bond and I was released only to find out two weeks later that I had a federal warrant out of St. Louis.   I turned myself in and was released three weeks later pending sentencing. My guideline range was twenty-four to thirty-six months federal prison and up to sixty months supervised release.   I started staying high because all my friends, or what I thought were friends, were giving me meth because they were not in jail because I didn't tell on them.

On April 1st, 2000, I turned myself in to the federal prison in Springfield, Mo.   I was there about a month and got a 101 assault (riot) with serious bodily injury.

I spent five months in the hole as it was called.   I asked for a priest and he came with the Lord's supper and a Bible.   I was transferred to a different prison and was just glad I didn't get anymore time added on.

My wife lost custody of my kids.   My parents got them.   I took all the classes in prison they said I should take.   I was released September 20th, 2001, only to be back in March of 2002.   My parents adopted my kids and over the course of eight years I would get on my feet for a year or two and get strung out, going to treatment only to repeat the cycle.   I ended up going to state prison for participating in manufacturing.   I went to treatment in prison and college and was planning on becoming a drug and alcohol counselor.   I was released and I have not been back to prison since I was released June 20th, 2010.

I started a company B&B Construction with the help of my AA sponsor.   I divorced my wife because it was way overdue.   I got into another relationship with a woman who had never been involved with anything like I had and didn't drink either.   Somewhere along the way, operating my company consumed me and I started hiring guys who used drugs and it wasn't long 'til I started smoking pot then I was using heroin which ended my three year relationship and my growing company.   So I went to the last secular treatment and while being there one of the counselors gave me a recovery Bible and my roommate was always trying to get me to read my Bible rather than the big book of AA.   When I completed treatment he had put some scriptures in my Bible to read. I decided to get baptized and go to church. I knew it was the only thing that was going to work but with no one to help or show me, I started using again off and on. I had seven months left on probation for driving while license revoked and I was offered a job remodeling hotels so I asked for a travel permit which the parole officer denied. I told her that I was going anyway because I needed to get away. She said, "Well, when you don't show up I'll know why."

I left for Flagstaff, AZ May 5th, 2014. I met a girl and started using meth off and on and my mouth got me kicked off the job. A new girl, L., asked me to go to church with her and her kids and mom and I would go. But the new company I worked for sent me on a job in California and I met people and started using meth every day. I took L. and her kids to meet my family back in Missouri for Christmas. I asked her to marry me. The year 2015 would be the worst I ever got on meth. I knew after the job in Palm Desert, California was done I was going to be laid off. I had a foreman from a hotel renovation company call me. He had gotten my name from another contractor that was on the job. He was offering me a foreman's position to run a five man crew that would start in October. I accepted the offer and he would call me and I would call him from time to time.

So when the job ended everyone was laid off. I went back to Flagstaff with L. and the kids. I could feel that things there weren't the same. I didn't realize how bad I had gotten. So after about three weeks I found a job with a builder to go up to Boise, Idaho to frame and hang drywall.   So off I went and I was there about two weeks.   I met a girl outside the hotel I was staying at.   I was smoking some pot and in about ten minutes I was off with her.   The place she took me, the guy was really out there.   She got her stuff and stayed with me, of course.   She had meth so I was using and going to work while she would hustle drugs and herself all day.   That lasted about a month and she left to go back to California where she was from.   The same night her guy called me and asked if I was in need of some speed and I was, plus the guys I was working with wanted some too.

I got a call from a previous employer to go back to Palm Desert, California to finish off seven rooms and do what we call change outs and repairs.   I started shooting up meth again and it got bad.   I was hearing noises and would find myself scared to death in a room by myself.   I didn't know what was going on at the time.   So I went back to Flagstaff for about a week at L.'s and then back to Palm Desert.   I stayed with the superintendent and the same day we hooked up with the painters and there was more meth.   The superintendent and I both stayed high.   I quit shooting up and smoked my life away.   The job was only going to last a month or so.   When I left the job I bought an ounce of meth thinking I could just sell it until this job in October was to come up in three months.

The night I got back to Flagstaff things went all bad. L.'s boy was throwing one of his fits and the cops got called.   When they showed up they asked for an ID. I knew that I had missed a couple of court dates for assault and disorderly conduct.   I knew the meth was not in my luggage but I had some on me.   They searched me and didn't find it and I couldn't believe it. His hand skipped right over my sock with a pipe and about four grams of meth in it.   They put me in the back seat of the car.   I managed to get the meth by slipping my hands under my feet and tried to eat it.   I chewed up the big chunks of it but knew I couldn't swallow it.   So I waited for it to turn into liquid to spit it out.   I barely remember the officer asking me what I had done and if I was alright.   I was very incoherent and they knew.   I was charged with possession of dangerous drug paraphernalia and introduction into a controlled facility.   I was set to go to court that next week.   I really thought I was going back to prison with these charges so a day later I pled guilty to the assault and disorderly conduct.   I was going to have to wait fourteen days for sentencing on that.   Wednesday came and no court.   The guys in there with me said don't say nothing.   Maybe they lost the paperwork.   It didn't get filed.   So fourth of July I asked one of the co-officers if they could let me know when I had court.   Just the one date so I asked what my bond was.   They said fifteen-hundred cash. I called my mom and told her that my bond was only fifteen-hundred dollars cash and not seventy-eight hundred anymore.   She knew what it was and after having a long talk I told her to call this bondsman I found and get me out, that I was coming back home as soon as I went to court.   They posted my bond and I was released.

I didn't leave Flagstaff for another three months almost to the day. On October 5th, 2015, I had talked to BK from S&A and he needed me to work in Hilton Head, SC so off to South Carolina. I was to meet a guy in St. Louis and he was going with me. He never showed up to pick me up. So I called a friend, C., who I had lived at an Oxford house with and he came and got me and the plan was to just work for the rest of the year and to catch up with BK at the first of the year. Come to find out the guy that was supposed to meet me in St. Louis was having a triple bi-pass. BK understood and I didn't have a car so we would meet up after New Years' for the South Carolina job.

So C. had been using again too and he was very unpredictable. But he started calling companies to sub-contract for and he found one. I realized right away that these salesmen were not good ones so I got hold of my old contacts that I knew would have roofs or siding to do to stay busy. I left Illinois on probation and quit reporting. On November 8th, I was arrested and taken to jail. My lawyer wouldn't answer my calls so I was sentenced to forty-five days.

I had no idea I had been Jesus-jacked. I knew in my heart God was telling me there was a better way of life. I remembered this recovery Bible I had been carrying around with me so I went to church. I couldn't hold back the tears as I told the pastor about my mom's liver transplant and that I had been praying for perserverance through whatever was to happen. I told him all about my problems with drugs and he told me about Mission Teens and that I should pray and seek God's answer.   I knew that it was what I needed to do.   When I went back to church, I got a newsletter from First Fruits in Jerseyville.   I read in it a testimony about a girl that had stayed to do overseeing.   I prayed to God to give me answers.   I was reading the 12 and 12 of AA, the 11th month.   As I was reading, when I got to the end of the chapter, the last sentence said, 'This will be the first fruits of your spiritual life.'   I knew at that point I needed to get my life right with God.

So I told my family that I had tried everything possible to live right and it never worked out so I got to give God an opportunity to help me with my problem. Now I had this great idea to get into Mission Teens. But I had the thought that if I got out of jail and my tools were still at the job after my forty-five day stay, I could work through the first of the year and if I was still not doing well I would go to Mission Teens.   I was released two days early and C. was even more crazy from his drug use and I knew that things were going to get worse.   My tools were gone so I was real limited to my choices.   I really did not understand how everything got this bad and every door of opportunity slammed shut.   I still had BK to fall on but without any tools.   How could I explain showing up at a job site with no tools.   BK called.   I told him the problem and he said no problem, he said he would help me get tools and he would call me back with all the info to where I would be going.   So my living arrangements at C.'s came to an end because he was talking to the TV and he thought it was talking back to him.

I went to another friend's and called God's New Life in Marked Tree, AR and was accepted. I worked for the next four days with M., my old sponsor, to get money for a bus ticket and my frozen money to get to St Louis, MO. I needed to get my blood work done so I bought my ticket to leave January 18th, 2016, but on Monday I had to get my blood work and couldn't. Now J., my ex-wife's cousin, (where I was staying) started acting really crazy when I came back from the hospital. So I called M., my sponsor, and tried to get to the bus station to catch the bus and come without the blood work just to get away from the craziness that seemed to happen to everyone I got around. I missed the bus so I was out of a ticket and when I got back to J.'s he was beating up a fifty year old man. I stopped him and left, called the police and told them so they would stop it.

While I was standing outside of a little corner store going through my phone to find a place to stay, almost no money, and not sure how I was going to get another bus ticket and blood work, a friend, who was a sales guy for a roofing company I sub-contracted for showed up. He said, "Is that you B.?" I said, "Yes." He asked how I had been doing. I just said not well and that I was strung out and was trying to get into an eight to ten month program. He asked if I had any money. I said very little. I was more concerned with where I was going to stay. I called A., the only person I knew who lived a Christian life to see if he was home. He was three blocks away. He was home and told me to come by.   We could talk. When I hung up my friend was just standing there looking at me with sad eyes.   He said, "Here B., get some help."   And handed me what looked like a folded up dollar bill and walked away before I could say anything.   It turned out to be a one-hundred dollar bill.   A. was and is a blessed man.   He welcomed me to stay until I got the blood work.

I left St. Louis at eight p.m., January 21st, 2015.   I had never in all my life had such a sense of peace.   It was the greatest feeling.   My heart and soul was crying out for the living God and to be real honest I didn't even know what was going on.   I arrived here in Marked Tree, AR at ten-forty a.m., January 22nd, 2015. I have learned so much about God's love for me.   I used to have questions to God about why I had to go through so much and He has answered me through Psalms 119:71.   "It is good for me that I have been afflicted; that I might learn thy statutes."

I have graduated the eight to ten month program. God has done a work in me all because I waved the white flag of surrender to Him and I trust Him with my life today.   I never knew what or why Jesus is so important for us who believe in Him and Him willingly going to the cross, dying for our sins, resurrected on the third day, and seated at the right hand of God and one day He will come back for us.   I have stayed here because I have made up my mind to help others like myself so I can pour out what was poured out into me.

I have completed my AC committment and have

become a full counselor.   I really don't think that the title of it is as important as it is to just be part of building the kingdom of Heaven.   John 15:5 says, "I am the vine, ye are the branches: He that abideth in me, and I in him, the same bringeth forth much fruit: for without me ye can do nothing."

My life is a living example of what happens apart from Him.   I never want to go back to that so I have chosen to remain in Him.   Amen.   B.D.B.

*

When I read the first part of B.D.B's life I was so saddened for him.   I absolutely cannot stand to hear about child abuse of any kind.   This man had it pretty rough as a kid.   I was thrilled that someone finally helped him.   The beatings from his father made B.D.B. defensive and prompted him to fight with others, the only life he had known-to fight back. And seeing his mother go through all of it too. What a nightmare!

It sounds like he was basically on his own most of his young life which forced him to learn the way of the world quickly and how to survive.   He never really had much parental guidance but thank God for his mother giving him what she could.   B.D.B. was never settled down for very long.   Always hopping around from place to place, in and out of relationships, in and out of trouble.   How he must have longed for peace and contentment.   You can read it between the lines.   Never having a stable, loving home life, he yearned for it, sought it but never found it.   Until God started to deal with him, until God began a process of calling his name, starting out at just a whisper, a yearning in B.D.B.'s soul.   Then God began sending messengers to help him get to his destination.   God has people ready to heed the call and He puts them in the right place at just the right time to help the one that God has His sights on.   God wanted to save B.D.B. from the life that he was living and B.D.B. realized that surrendering to God was the only way he was going to break the chains, the memories of horrid abuse, the sorrow in his soul.   Praise God, B.D.B. now belongs to that great innumerable heavenly host of Almighty God.   He is helping others to break those binding chains too.   Not only is he-to reverse the saying here-walking it, but he is also talking it to those still lost in the pit of addiction.   God can always use another good man!

LIFE STORY #5

Female, 44 years of age

My name is S.R. and I am forty-four years old and this is my story.   I had a great childhood for which I have no complaints.   My mother and father were divorced when I was two.   I have two sisters.   I am the youngest.   We lived with my mom and step-dad in Piedmont, Missouri and stayed with my grandma and dad on weekends and during the summer.   I had the best momma and dad and most wonderful grandmas you have ever seen.   My grandmas were the ones that took us to church from the time we were born. So I knew about God from the beginning although I didn't really understand but I always had Jesus next to me.

My step-dad was very strict but he truly had only the best intentions although as children we didn't see that. We called him Hitler. Ha. For instance we lived on a rock hill and he made us pick up a wheelbarrow full of rocks just to move them over across the hill to another place.   To this day, I hate wheelbarrows. Ha.   I was very outgoing in school.   I played the saxophone from fifth grade to eighth and I was first chair.   I loved it. I played volleyball, basketball, and softball.   I started in all three when I was a freshman.   I played on the varsity team (basketball) and we went to State.   It was so cool.

When I turned fifteen I moved from Piedmont to Doniphan, Missouri to live with my dad.   This was about the time I started getting into drinking and smoking marijuana.   Since I was on the basketball team and I did have a curfew, it was touch and go with my new habits-just every now and then.   My step-dad drank Busch beer so I used to sneak it out and meet my friends down the road then sneak back in. At my dad's, the weekends are when I would drink and smoke but had a good high school life.   I got awards for most school spirit and made A's, B's, and C's.

I was a senior and met my son's dad and fell madly in love with him.   He was a dealer and user of speed. This is where I started using meth a lot.   He would pick me up from my basketball games and we would just ride.   One night we drove from Doniphan to St. Louis, twice in one night which is a three and a half hour trip one way.   At this time, I became addicted to meth.   I was a starter on the basketball team.   I was a senior at the time and I would tell my dad I was staying with a friend and I would go with D.   But we would stay up all night and then I would go to school and then go play a game.   It didn't seem to matter with my playing although I'm sure it did.   Halfway through the season I found out I was pregnant.   I was obsessed with playing basketball and D. was kind of wild-not to mention he was twenty-seven, I was seventeen-so we decided on an abortion.   This is the first thing in my life that I realize now started me on a downward spiral.   But wait.   I left out one other thing.   I had fallen deeply, madly in love at age thirteen through sixteen and got my heart broken by my first love.   He was the one that introduced me to marijuana.   When we broke up is when I met D.

Okay, so I had made an appointment to get an abortion in St. Louis but when I got there they took me in this room and showed me a video of how they kill the babies.   I ran out screaming at them, "Why would you show me that?"   They grabbed my arm and tried to keep me from leaving.   They had tricked me when I called.   I had really made an appointment with an anti-abortion place.   They were highly against abortion.   It was truly one of the most traumatic experiences that I had been through.   Needless to say, we stayed the night and I did go through with it the next day-which to this day, this haunts me.   I have asked the Lord forgiveness for this since I have been here at Teen Mission and I know I am forgiven for I was young and didn't know what I was doing.   I do regret this decision I had made.   If I could do things all over again, I would never do it.   But I realize now I don't have to suffer with the guilt of this anymore.   I am forgiven.

So I graduated and moved in with D.   First time I ever lived away from my home.   Five months after I graduated, I got pregnant again.   I was keeping this baby for sure.   It was a boy.   I quit using any type of drug during my pregnancy.   I found out when I was five months pregnant that D. also had another woman pregnant.   My world was crushed.   But I stayed with him and we raised my son until he was four.

Then we broke up and I got with my second son's dad, R.   I got pregnant again and both times I was pregnant I quit using drugs.   So both my babies were very healthy.   But when my second son was two, R. and I lost him to his grandmother because she knew we were using drugs.   It was truly the most difficult thing I have ever experienced.   I longed for my son every day and every night.   This is when I started using the needle.   I was completely and utterly out of mind.   I miss him so bad that I once almost committed suicide.   I was driving down the highway and crying and was in total despair.   A semi was coming toward me and I was so close to almost just swerving out in front of it that I actually saw it happen, then at the last second I pulled over and just wept on the side of the road.   I tried everything to get him back.   Me and R. stayed together for two years after she took him, trying together to get him back. But eventually we both collapsed under the pressure of trying to please everyone and jumping through hoops.   Meanwhile, my son was wanting his momma and daddy so bad and he wouldn't eat.   She had to give him supplements because at age three he had big black rings around his eyes.   He was skinny.   He cried for me all the time.   My heart was completely broken.   I continued to go deeper into the world of meth which is a dark evil place.   Me and his dad both were on a path going the same way the devil was going.   I promise you at this time I saw a different realm, a realm where not all traveled.   I was playing with fire.   It was during this time me and my youngest son's dad eventually broke up.

I met my husband.   He is a man of God and of great faith.   He brought me out of the depths of despair and I got saved and baptized.   Both my boys loved him.   He was kind.   But he and I also used meth together and he was a cook.   So I had meth right in front of me at all times.

My youngest son's grandma died when he was seven. And me and his dad shared him but this is the time I started going to jails and prison.   I ended up doing four prison sentences, all for drugs.   I missed my oldest son's high school graduation on my last term in prison which was two and a half years.   I also missed his junior and senior basketball games.   You have to understand ever since he was little basketball was our life.   We played constantly all the way through high school.   I practiced with him and his best friend J. To miss these games was one of the most horrible feelings I had felt while sitting in prison.

My younger son's dad, R., kept him with a steady home while I was at prison.   I missed out on a lot with him. But his dad was a good dad.   He drank too much but he was good.   He just got killed three years ago in a horrible wreck which I struggle with to this day. Since I have been at Mission Teens I have had three dreams of him which if you would've ask me the day I got here what I wanted, it would have been to find Jesus and have Him come into my life so I never have to go back where I was and to be able to have a dream about R.   Just last night I had a dream about him and I told him, "Wait a minute, wait a minute.   I better hurry and tell you something since I only have so long in this dream."   And I looked straight at him and said with the most heartfelt words I could muster and looked right into his eyes and said, "I miss you."   And he smiled back with that little crooked grin he had and I woke up bawling, but tears of joy.

After my last prison term I prayed to God and God has answered my prayers.   It has been six years now that I have been to prison and I am in Mission Teens learning about how Jesus was born to come back and save us.   I have always known God and read my Bible but until I got here I never really knew the Word and never knew it was a way of living.   This is what I had been missing out on-a true relationship with God. When I walked in here I was sick as I could be and they were like well, pray about it.   I thought they were crazy but since I have been here I have learned to trust in Jesus and to live by His words and to go out on that limb to have faith.

He has blessed me beyond anything I could ever imagine and know by being obedient to Him only good things are to come.   This place has truly changed my words, my actions, my life.   Thank you, Jesus.   Thank you, Mission Teens.

*

Peer pressure is a top reason that kids start using drugs.   In S.R.'s case, the boyfriend at the age of thirteen.   And it always seems to be marijuana or alcohol first.   Listed below are some of the top reasons kids try drugs/alcohol--

Other People-friends, parents, other relatives or adults do drugs.

Popular Media-glamorization of drugs or alcohol in television/movies.

Escape and Self-Medication-pressures of school, social relationships.

Boredom-nothing to do, left alone, crave excitement and activity.

Rebellion-anger at parents, being misunderstood.

Instant Gratification-the "I want it now" generation. Drugs work fast.

Lack of Confidence-drugs reduce inhibitions, shyness or awkwardness.

Misinformation-friends who are "experts" and will inform you wrongly.

I know this is such a cliché but when I was a kid we didn't have time to think about what friends or others were doing, didn't have time to watch much television and sure couldn't afford to go to a movie. We just had to "suck it up" or "cry it out" if there was school pressure or a girlfriend/boyfriend relationship that didn't work out.   We weren't bored at all because we were working on homework or in a field or farm, which is the main reason we stayed out of trouble and away from the "bad" things that were going on around us.   And we never craved excitement or activity.   We were just tired and wanted to sleep.   There was no instant gratification-you worked for what you got and it took a long time to earn the money to buy it-nothing came fast.   Some inhibitions were good-that was your conscience.   If you were shy or awkward, you just grew out of it.   And every time we listened to a friend that told us something wrong, we got into trouble so we stopped listening to that friend. Amen? Amen.

S.R. said she had a great childhood but when she hit thirteen, the pressure to fit in hit her.   And she did like so many of us do, succumbed to that pressure which eventually led to many wrong decisions, including the very regrettable abortion.   All abortions are to be regretted.   Our lady in this story *did* regret her actions and prayed for forgiveness.

So much of her life was wasted, missing out on her children growing up, always getting involved with the wrong person, going to prison because of drugs. Satan is such a destroyer of everything that is good, isn't he?   But S.R. finally made the right choice, the one she had known about since childhood.   Her own words, "So I knew about God from the beginning."   She remembered the Jesus that her grandmothers took her to hear about.   And what does the Bible say about that?   "Train up a child in the way he should go: and when he is old, he will not depart from it."- Proverbs 22:6.

The Father, the Son and the Holy Spirit, all three in one, are somebody you won't likely forget.   Once you have heard the greatest news of all time you will remember it.   And in times of trouble you will cry out from the pit where your sins have dragged you down, "Dear God, save me lest I perish!"   S.R.

uttered those words, if not in voice then in her soul, and God heard her cry.   She now walks in the light and the newness of spirit.

She states that by being obedient to Him only good things are to come.   'Trust and obey, for there's no other way to be happy in Jesus, but to trust and obey'-as the old song of the church goes.   S.R. *will* make it through, *will* have a relationship with God, *will* live a thriving life.   The happiness in her words are evidence of God's love.

LIFE STORY #6

Male, 51 years of age

My name is S. P. and I am 51 years old at the time I write this.   I was born the first of three sons in the small town of Wynne, Arkansas on August 9th, 1965. Two years after me was born my brother, S., and another five years later, C.   My earliest memories include mostly my brother S. because we were so close in age.   These are also some of my best memories because my mom and dad were still married.   They both worked at full time jobs which means that S. and I spent a lot of time at the babysitter's.   I can remember them teaching us our alphabets and how to count there by the age of three or four years old.   But I can also remember seeing some of the kids there physically abused.   Nothing really serious I don't guess but plenty of switching, cleaning mouths out with soap and stuffing food into the mouths of babies as they cried.   That was probably the worst thing I saw.   Those poor little babies crying their heads off as someone was stuffing soup into their mouths choking them.   I never understood that.

I was probably around six or seven then during the summer when school was out.   During school time we just caught the bus home and stayed there until mom got home from work at around four or five p.m.   No one worried with locking doors in those days out in the country.   My brother S. and I were very close in those early years.   We did everything together.   We did all the normal things kids did at that age.   We made forts out of cane and sticks, played army, rough-housed in our rooms until we got in trouble and the like.

We moved into the house in the country when I was five years old.   I remember it well because we would get to visit the site as it was being built.   All of us as a family.   My mom actually drew up the plans for it and Mom and Dad picked the site to build and bought the land and hired carpenters to do the building.   We would go out on weekends and pick up sticks and limbs out of what would become the yard and to check on the progress of the house.   It was a beautiful rock and cypress three bedroom house.   We moved into it on August 8th, 1970.   I turned six years old the day after that.   I remember this because I chiseled it into the carport driveway and a brick, although I had the year wrong, I chiseled 1969.   We were living a nice upper middle class life style at that time.   We had nice furniture.   I remember getting a brand new Zenith television, console style, and we always had plenty to eat and decent clothes.   S. and I had lots of toys and eventually our own motorcycles to play on. We would all go out to eat at a restaurant from time to time and everything seemed to be as it should be. But then somewhere along the way things began to slowly change.   I'm not exactly sure when but I would say somewhere around the time my brother C. was born in 1972 or a year later.

There would be weekends that me and my brothers would load up into the car and drive around town usually by bars and hotels searching for my dad.   And there were nights that he would come home drunk and began arguing with Mom.   They would get into fights which scared us kids of course.   We couldn't understand what was going on at the time.   Years later I would come to understand that my dad was staying out all weekend partying with his friends, getting drunk and seeing other women.   I have long since forgiven him.   He regrets the mistakes he made back then even more than I do.   This progressed until my mom had finally had enough.   One day she packed us all up with as much as we could take in one car load and we left the house and my dad, never to return to this day.   I can remember writing a short letter saying goodbye to my dad.   This would be the beginning of a big turn around in my life.

From there we moved into a trailer park next to Wal-Mart in downtown Wynne.   My mom had actually started seeing someone else before she left my dad and they soon married.   Life in the trailer park was definitely different.   But most of this was because of having to adjust to the new family life.   My step-dad was a good man.   I have nothing bad to say about him.   One of the craziest things that I remember about living there is the way S. and I would play at Wal-Mart.   It was like our playground with all the toys we could ever want.   We spent hours there playing with whatever toys we wanted.   We would simply open them up and use them until we got ready to go home again.   But we never took anything out of the store.   And the employees, although they knew what we were doing, never said anything to us about it.   Things were far different back then.

We eventually moved into a new house in a better part of town when I was twelve years old.   This is when things really began to go downhill for me.   I met the next door neighbor who introduced me to things that I had never ever considered doing before.   I began smoking cigarettes at the age of thirteen along with drinking alcohol and smoking pot.   But the worse thing that I was introduced to was stealing.   I began with shoplifting.   We would ride our bikes downtown. We lived in the suburbs at this time and would go into stores pocketing small things like candy.   Then it was on to larger items.   It began more as a thrill than anything.   But little did I know I was feeding a monster that would grow and become the source of many problems in my life.

We were very soon sneaking out at night and breaking into buildings, burglarizing them.   We stole cigarettes, candy and any money we might find. Finally, still aged only thirteen years old we were caught and I went to jail for my first time.   I was there over the weekend and released to my dad.   I received a slap on the wrist and that was that.   But this didn't bring about any change in my behavior.   I just learned from my mistakes.   My drug use had also progressed during this time.   I had begun breaking into medical clinics to steal drugs and was caught doing this, too.   I received probation and was put on a twenty-four hour curfew.   I could only go to school

*without my parents.   Any other time I left my yard I
was supposed to be accompanied by them.   By the
time I was sixteen I had already tried LSD,
barbiturates,   opiates,   psilocybin   mushrooms,
benzodiazepines, and marijuana.   The pot was on a
daily basis by now.*

*I had always been very interested in science and so I
took chemistry during my eleventh grade.   I was
fascinated by the way compounds combined and
interacted to form completely new compounds.   I
also had a physician's desk reference and studied it to
learn the names of all the "good" drugs, both the
brand names and the generic names.   I also had
become very interested in how to make LSD.   I had
several books on chemistry and had filled a notebook
with notes on how it was obtained from ergot and
certain chemicals.   So I devised a plan to get the
chemicals I needed by breaking in and stealing them
from my high school laboratory.   I decided to make a
homemade bomb using muzzle loading gunpowder.
I started a small fire after loading all the lab supplies
into my step-dad's truck after sneaking out in it.   I
left the dynamite I had made for the fire to reach
hoping the explosion would appear to be a chemical
accident but it went out before reaching it.   It was
about three weeks later that the lab equipment, etc,
was discovered in my bedroom at home by the police.
They were actually searching for evidence of another
crime a friend and I had committed.   I eventually
received a five year prison sentence for this.   I turned
seventeen a few weeks after getting there.   I was
released after serving ten months, got my first full*

time job in a factory and got married at eighteen years old.   My marriage lasted only about two years because my wife and I were both doing drugs and drinking through it all.   We were both arrested during that time also.

After the divorce, I began to party and run around quite a bit and ended up getting four DWI's in a two year period.   The third was reduced to DWI 1 and the fourth was DWI 2.   That's the only reason I didn't get into more trouble than a few days in jail and fines. But my parole officer found out and I had my parole violated and went back to prison for six months.   I ended up getting out with my sentence completed.

I worked that summer and began pursuing college by taking the ACT test.   I scored high enough to get a full scholarship to three different colleges and ended up going to Arkansas State University in Jonesboro, AR.   I did pretty good starting out but as always began hanging out with the wrong crowd, partying almost every night and drinking far too much.   I slowly began missing classes because I was too hung over to go.   I was pretty irresponsible to say the least. I finished my freshman year of college and met a girl over the summer.   By the time I started my sophomore year of college we had become serious. Then after only two or three weeks into that semester I got another DWI.   This one on campus.   I decided to pack my things up and leave college.

I went back to work at the same factory and got married to my second wife not long after that.   Our *relationship started out bad from the beginning because though I did care for her and fell in love with her I was using her at the same time.   She stole pain pills from her mom who was at one time a nurse and knew many other people that had them.   She didn't ever use at that time but gave them all to me.   I got in trouble with the law again in our first year together, this time for fraud and forgery.   I was writing prescriptions and getting them filled in several different towns.   I was finally caught in Jonesboro and got three years probation.   My addiction to narcotics slowly got worse and worse over the next five years.   I was by this time burglarizing medical clinics, veterinarian clinics, and a pharmacy.   I got away with this for over four years but was caught and received a ten year sentence in prison.   My wife stuck by me through it all or so I thought.   When I made parole and told her I was coming home soon, she broke the news that she had been seeing someone else. After thinking it over and realizing it was all my fault I told her that I was willing to forgive her and work it out.   But she wanted to see me and him both until she decided what she wanted.   So I told her that she had already made her decision then.   So we eventually divorced not long after.*

I began doing a lot of narcotics and methamphetamine during this time, living in what seemed like a perpetual hell.   After only eight months out on parole I went back on a parole violation for a dirty urinalysis.   I ended up doing over one and a half years because one of the stipulations was that I must complete a nine month therapeutic community program before my release.   Upon being released after finishing the program I remained clean for only a short time before falling back into my drug addiction.   I was so used to that life style that I couldn't ever imagine anything different much less believe I could have a better life.   So needless to say, I ended up getting another parole violation.   I was in prison another year and a half before getting out once again.

This time, instead of returning to my home town, I took my brother up on his offer to parole out to him in Harrison, Arkansas.   I lived with him until I got a job and my own apartment.   I lived in Harrison for a little over a year when my brother, who was a physician there, offered me the opportunity of moving with him to Fredericksburg, Virginia where he was beginning his own practice as a surgeon.   His offer was for me to be his new office manager there.   I accepted with both gratitude and some reservations. I guess that you could say I had lost much of my self confidence over the years because of my past life style. So I moved to Virginia with him and we began his new practice.   Things went well the first few months and I injured my back and I was prescribed percocet.   I was right back into my addiction and began using my position at the office to obtain more narcotics by forgery and fraud.   This went on for over four months until I was finally caught and sent to jail.   I eventually received a sixteen month sentence in prison and served thirteen months of it.

After being released I went back to work at a local

factory.   I worked there about a year and then moved back to Arkansas.   Within three years I was not only addicted to opiates but had been introduced to manufacturing of methamphetamine.   Now I was finally beginning to come to the end of myself.   I had been to several rehabs throughout my life but always for the wrong reason.   I went for the courts and went to keep a job for my wife and for my family but never for myself until now.   I was facing two Class Y felonies, one for manufacturing and one for possession of meth with intent to deliver.   When the judge said that both carried a term of imprisonment of ten years to forty years to life, he definitely got my attention. When I went to court all I had going for me was a lengthy criminal record and a court appointed lawyer. I say this with sarcasm of course.   Things didn't look good for me at all but after finishing my first faith-based rehab called Project New Start, I was beginning to try and trust the Lord and to keep a positive attitude.

And God came through for me in a big way.   I thought I would get at least the ten year sentence but got only five years probation instead and on top of that I made the decision to ask the court a month later to drop twenty-five hundred dollars in old fines and to reinstate my driver's license and they did!   Only because I told the judge with sincerity that I had God in my life and needed help in starting my life again.

Things were beginning to look better until I compromised and I did some meth again.   After a few weeks of weekend use I realized I was headed for disaster once again and decided to go to Mission Teens. This was the best, most important decision I have ever made. I know that I had been running from God my whole life without realizing it.

It's been a continual journey of learning to know who the Lord is and at the same time learning to know who I really am. The first thing God had to heal me of was shame, guilt and condemnation. But thankfully, this took only a couple of weeks or so. After that He began working on those things that I don't believe we ever finish working on totally. We only grow better in them. These things are my self worth and self confidence, not because of what I've done but because of what He has done and made possible for me to do through His strength. He has also helped me in being more obedient to His word.

I have more control of anger, though I'm far from arriving at the place I'd like to be. I'm learning to love others more and more by being more patient, more understanding and open minded to the fact that God is working on them like He did me. I don't know the pain they feel or have lived through and I don't know how far God has already brought them so I try to remember that He is in control. I am amazed at how much my eyes have been opened to some of the spiritual truths revealed to me so far. Yet, I know there is so much more in store for me.

*

Two failed marriages, numerous stints in prisons, several chances at making a better life for himself-one for a college education and a really good one with his brother, a surgeon.   He was very intelligent.   How could S.P. have blown it all?   The early divorce of his parents created a void, emotionally and financially for him and his brothers. They went from a nice home and having plenty to living in a trailer park and trying to deal with a new father figure.   Those things as I stated in a previous story, are hard on a child.   It is not stated in his story but it sounds like he had little supervision and he and his brothers could do pretty much what they wanted which included roaming around town. When kids are allowed to do that, there is usually trouble waiting for them.   They will find just about anything to occupy their time and especially if they have a buddy to do it with.

But what made S.P. go in the wrong direction?   One of his brothers went in a very right direction. Nothing is stated about the youngest brother. Resentment over the divorce and the lost "good life", unresolved anger?   He was the oldest and was impacted more than the other brothers perhaps.   I can only make guesses, I am way far from being a psychologist.

S.P. knows why he did all these things.   He lived through the hurt and anger, the stealing and the drugs.   Then one day he came to that realization that he could not keep doing what he was doing-that it was a dead-end street, literally.   Before he lapsed back into the old way of living, he called out for help, the right kind of help.

I can't explain God.   But I do know He is a life-changing force.   The evidence is real and cannot be denied.   S.P. knows this as well as everyone who has come into the presence of God.   One can only bow to the will of God and accept Him as Lord. There are many who are proud and filled with self worth, going their own way and boasting that they will never be constricted to a religion that demands worship of some god, little g.   But when you come into contact with God, big G, you *will* bow your knees, you *will* submit to His will, you *will* realize the error of your prideful ways.   Because you can do none else but that.   The Bible says, "EVERY knee shall bow, EVERY tongue shall confess that Jesus Christ is Lord."   That is stated in the book of Philippians and Revelation where it speaks of the future return of Christ.   But I think it applies to everyone in the present tense-at the very moment a person feels that twinge, that calling, that whisper of God.   You instantly know and are convicted of your sins, your disobedience to God and shame overwhelms you.   You are humbled before God and you will bow your knee to Him.   Like someone who is in tremendous physical pain will do ANYTHING, take ANY medicine if there is a chance it will stop the pain.   God is that pain killer!   Try Him, free of charge, one-hundred percent guaranteed to work.

S.P. knew he needed God.   God was his only hope. He has just begun his walk with God.   Stick with God, S.P.   He will stick closer to you than those brothers of yours that you loved.

LIFE STORY #7

Female, 63 years of age

It's Christmas Eve.   I have so much to be thankful for. For the last nine Christmas Eve's, I have been clean and sober.   To God be the glory.

As I sit here across from my ninety-one year old dad, the love of my life, I realize just how blessed I have been my entire life.   There was no lack of love in our house so what happened to me for me to become so lost and addicted?   There are probably a million answers to that question but it certainly was not because of not being loved, not being raised right and not having wonderful parents.

I was born in 1954.   Momma had my name picked out for awhile,   my first name B., because she loved it, my middle name, I., was after my grandmother.   I have two brothers and one sister.

There was always a lot of laughter in our home, church every Sunday, church camp in the summer and great family vacations, the perfect childhood.

When I turned eighteen I pretty much thought I was grown.   Which I was not, far from it.   I was introduced to pot, everyone was doing it.   The late 60's and 70's seemed so glamorous to me.   The

Vietnam war was ending, the civil rights movement, women's liberation, the music.   I fell in love with concerts and parties.

I had a chance to go to southern California and I took it.   It was so different than Arkansas.   I seemed to fit right in.   I wanted to experience everything.

When I look back at that time in my young life I know I must have had many people praying for me.   The Lord kept me safe and out of harms way.   What started out glamorous and exciting ended up being very much the opposite, dark and dangerous.

I met my son's father, J., after I had been in California about a year and a half.   We got married and soon moved back to Arkansas.   I woke up one morning and he was gone-went back to California.   Of course, I ran back to him.   Things were good, so I thought, for a year.   We found out that I was pregnant.   I just knew things were going to work out.   After my son was born, J. introduced me to cocaine.   I knew from the first time it was not a good thing.   I was ready to come home.   California was not where I wanted to raise my son.

So here we go, back to Arkansas.   We got a house and a car.   Things seemed great then it all came crashing down.   I had known that J. had struggled with heroin at one time but had no idea he had picked it back up again.   He did a great job hiding it from me.   I packed up my son and moved in with my parents. We never saw or heard from him again, ever.

Bad relationships, divorce, becoming a single parent wasn't how I thought my life would be.   Trying to fill an emptiness inside with drugs is how I chose to exist. Things only got darker.   The really sad part about it is I knew better.

I've never met an addict that lived happily ever after and I have known many.   Jail, prison and death is how that life ends.   Bridges burned, families hurt, and life opportunities destroyed.   I thank God today that I had praying grandparents and praying parents. God heard their prayers.

After I had lost everything over and over again, I decided I was done.   I really was sick and tired.   I cried out to God, "Is this all there is for me, Lord?"

Very shortly after that, I found out about Mission Teens.   I knew that this was life or death for me.   I probably had another relapse in me but I knew I didn't have another recovery.   This was it.   No matter how many wrong decisions I had made in the past, how much I had lost, His love embraced me and set me free. I began to realize that I wasn't in control of anything.

Having a real relationship with the Lord Jesus Christ had given me freedom.   Freedom from addiction, the guilt and all the lies of the enemy.   The Lord continues to make me into an extraordinary new creation, renewing me day by day.   Today I want to believe that my purpose needs to match His purpose for me.

Being in Mission Teens changed my life.   It was my destiny.   For eight and a half years it has been my life.   By God's grace I have chosen not to give up.   I just keep moving until my head hits the pillow at night.

It's not about me anymore.   We begin to love others who are suffering.   We allow God to love others through us.   That's what Mission Teens is about-a relationship with Him so we can share that relationship with everyone.   Our Father has given us another chance because He desired a relationship with us.   Jesus' ministry, crucifixion, and his resurrection is everything we believe in.   Hallejuhah!

I am so very grateful for Jim Bracken's obedience, the founder of Mission Teens and I am so grateful for the wonderful family this ministry has blessed me with.

In closing, I just want to say life has continued to show up since I've been in the Mission.   My mother passed away, friends have died and, at this time, my son is in prison for the third time.   My saving grace is my relationship with Jesus Christ, my rock, my hope and my strength.   He is the reason that I am still alive, more alive today than I have ever been.   Praise the Lord!   B.I.M.

Psalms 40:1,2,3--I waited patiently and expectantly for the Lord and He inclined to me and heard my cry. He drew me up out of a horrible pit, (a pit of tumult and of destruction) out of the miry clay and set my feet upon a rock, steadying my steps and establishing

*my goings and he has put a new song in my mouth, a
song of praise to our God....*

*

This woman has her act together now.   You notice
she never really says what she had been addicted to.
And doesn't need to name it because what does it
matter?   Drugs, alcohol-any or all-it's all the same,
Satan's way of destroying another life by whatever
means he can.

She doesn't blame anyone or any circumstance but
takes full responsibility for her actions.   Another
thing, she came from a very loving home, a solid
foundation to pattern her life by.   Of course, getting
involved with a person who apparently did not have
her or his child's best interest at heart was definitely
straying onto the wrong road.   I took a wrong turn
on that road, too.

But God loves us even when we stray onto that
wrong road.   He sees the danger we are in and He
protects us until we find our way back onto the right
path.   He gently leads us along until we are
corrected.   His love is unfathomable, meaning one
can never find an end to it, there is no stopping
point.

B.I.M. has made a life for herself serving and guiding
others back to the correct path.   No doubt she has
seen many hard cases, lost some, gained some.   It
must be continually heartbreaking to see someone
you have been praying with, leading along, and

helping through the rough patches just to see them fall away and disappear into the black hole once again. It takes a strong person to stay with this kind of program. No doubt she is on her knees in constant prayer for those sent her way. But who prays for her? Let us hope that many people are praying for B.I.M. Let us be part of that group to support her.

EARLY MARKETING ADS

Early marketing advertisements of powerful drugs for medicinal purposes-hard to believe now when we read these. However, they were quite the norm when they were first introduced for public consumption. Generations were initiated into life with these substances so it is little wonder why the use of drugs is now at epidemic proportions.

Cocaine:

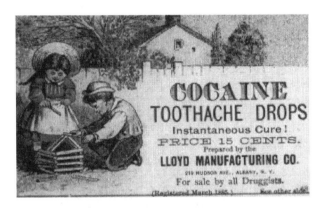

Lloyd Cocaine Toothache Drops
In the US, cocaine was sold over the counter until 1914 and was commonly found in products like toothache drops, dandruff remedies and medicinal tonics.

Metcalf's Coca Wine
Coca wine combined wine with cocaine, producing a compound now
known as coca ethylene, which, when ingested, is nearly as powerful a
stimulant as cocaine.

Vin Mariani Wine
The marketing efforts for coca wine focused primarily on its medicinal
properties, in part because it didn't taste very good and in part because
the coca ethylene effects were perceived to "fortify and refresh body
and brain" and "restore health and vitality.

Heroin:

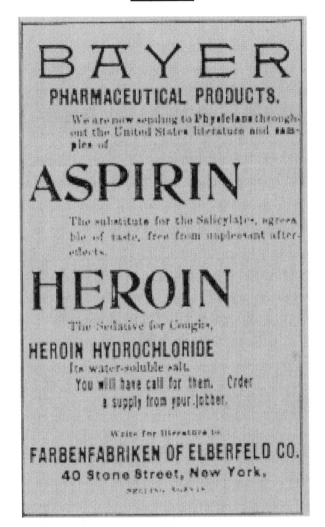

Bayer Heroin
From 1898 through to 1910, heroin was marketed as a cough
suppressant by trusted companies like Bayer — alongside the
company's other new product, Aspirin.

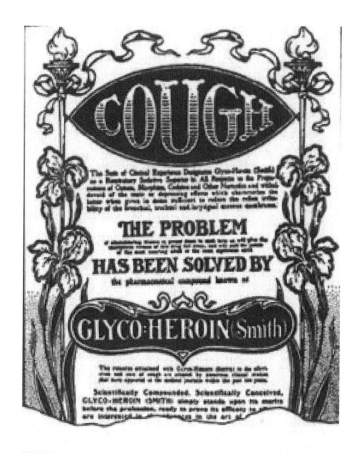

Smith Glyco-Heroin
A mixture of heroin and glycerin. "No other preparation has had its
therapeutic value more thoroughly defined or better established.

Opium:

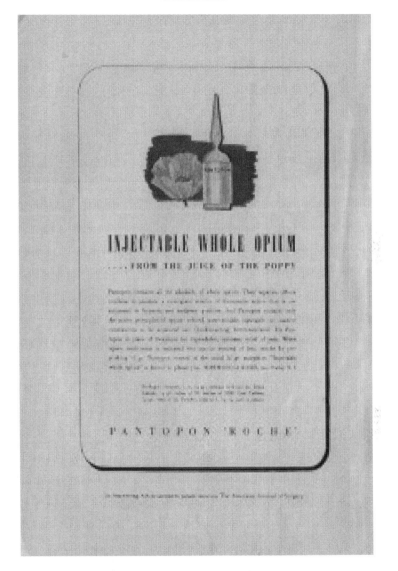

Pantopon Roche Injectable Opium
"Try Pantopon in place of morphine for dependable, optimum relief of pain.

Morphine:

Ayer's Cherry Pectoral
Depending on which list of contents you reference, this cure for colds,
coughs and "all diseases of the throat and lungs" contained either
morphine or heroin.

Mrs. Winslow's Soothing Syrup
Contained 65 mg of morphine per fluid ounce. "For children teething".

Quaaludes:

Quaalude-300
Brand name for the now-illegal sedative methaqualone. "Now the physician has one less tired, sleepy and apprehensive patient to contend with."

Cigarettes:

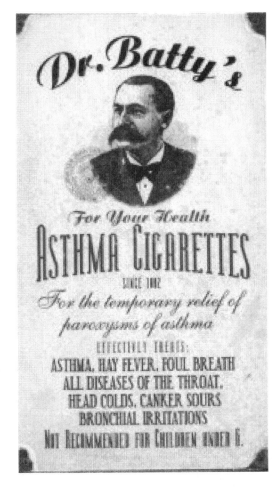

Dr. Batty's Asthma Cigarettes
Cigarettes with unknown contents claimed to provide temporary relief of
everything from asthma to colds, canker sores and bad breath. "Not
recommended for children under 6".

Alcohol:

Anheuser-Bush's Malt-Nutrine
Starting in the late 1800s, many breweries produced "food tonics," malt
beverages containing around 2% alcohol that were promoted as "food
in liquid form," aiding in digestion, increasing appetite and aiding in
sleep. "A boon to nursing mothers."

Pabst Extract
A malt tonic from Pabst. "The best tonic prepares the way for happy,
healthy motherhood".

Chloroform:

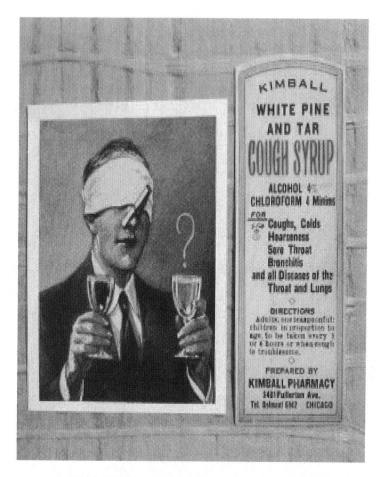

Kimball White Pine and Tar Cough Syrup
Until 1976, chloroform was used in consumer products like cough
syrup, toothpastes, ointments and other pharmaceuticals.

Marijuana:

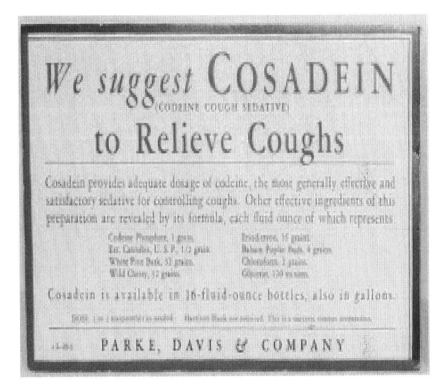

Cosadein
This cough remedy contained, among other things, codeine, chloroform
and cannabis.

<u>Soda:</u>

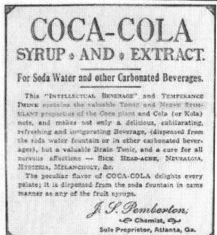

Coca-Cola
Coca-Cola was invented in the late 1800s as a "coca wine" (see above)
mix of wine and cocaine, but the alcohol and cocaine were later
replaced with syrup and coca leaves, respectively. Nevertheless,
typical coca wine claims of increased vitality remained for many years.
"A valuable brain tonic, and a cure for all nervous affections — sick
head-ache, neuralgia, hysteria, melancholy".

Amphetamines:

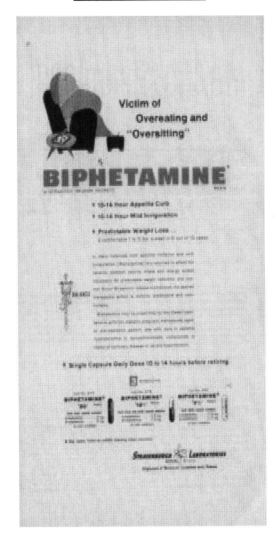

Biphetamine
A combination of two amphetamines; known popularly as "black
beauties." Marketed for its weight loss benefits.

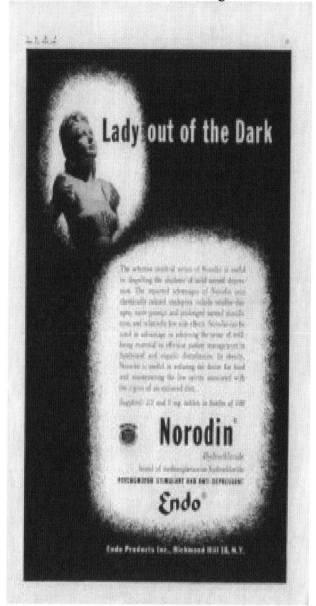

Norodin
Brand name for methamphetamine. "The selective cerebral action of
Norodin is useful in dispelling the shadows of mild mental depression.

Dexedrine
Brand name for dextroamphetamine. "Many of your patients —
particularly housewives — are crushed under a load of dull, routine
duties that leave them in a state of mental and emotional
fatigue…Dexedrine will give them a feeling of energy and well-being,
renewing their interest in life and living."

Barbiturates:

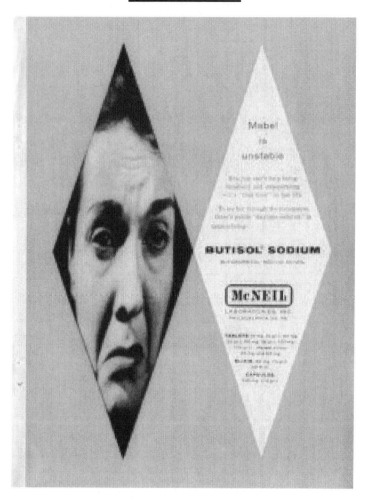

McNeil Butisol Sodium
Brand name for butabarbital. "Mabel is unstable… it's 'that time' in her
life. To see her through the menopause, there's gentle 'daytime
sedation' in Butisol Sodium.

Nembutal Suppositories
Brand name for pentobarbital. "When little patients balk at scary, disquieting examinations...When they need prompt sedation (and the oral route isn't feasible)...try Nembutal sodium suppositories...There is little tendency toward morning-after hangover."

Lakeside Pentobarbital and Phenobarbital
"When crisis demands quick-acting hypnotics".

<u>Unknown-Content Quackery:</u>

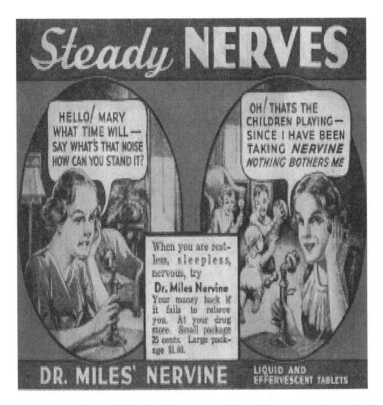

Dr. Miles' Nervine
"Since I have been taking Nervine, nothing bothers me."

Wolcott's Instant Pain Annihilator
"A speedy & permanent cure for headache, toothache, neuralgia,
catarrh and weak nerves."

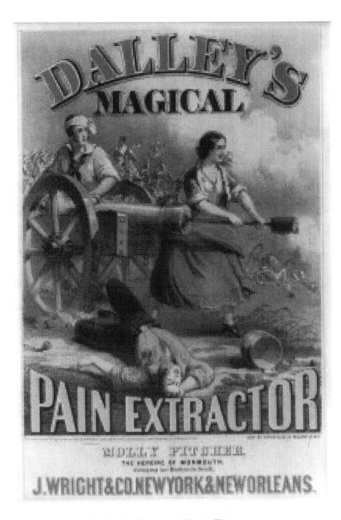

Dalley's Magical Pain Extractor
"Molly Pitcher, the heroine of Monmouth, avenging her husband's death."

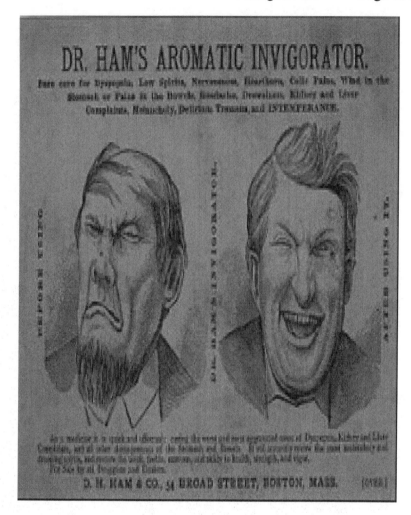

Dr. Ham's Aromatic Invigorator
A "cure for Dyspepsia, Low Spirits, Nervousness, Heartburn, Colic
Pains, Wind in the Stomach or Pains in the Bowels, Headache,
Drowsiness, Kidney and Liver Complaints, Melancholy, Delirium
Tremens, and Intemperance."

Source: http://www.pharmacytechs.net, Weed, Booze, Cocaine and
Other Old School "Medicine" Ads--by Mark Harris

MISSION TEENS

ABOUT MISSION TEENS

Mission Teens, Inc. is a non-denominational Christian Discipleship ministry dedicated to helping people who struggle with life-controlling problems by ministering the Gospel of Jesus Christ to them.   We believe that the Gospel should be free to all.

THE FOUNDER

Reverend James D. Bracken (1934-2012) founded Mission Teens, Inc. in 1969.   He opened the first residential center in Norma, NJ after much prayer.   He knew there was a need for a more effective ministry for the troubled young people who were attending his home prayer meetings. After two years of little results in the center, God answered his prayer by dictating to him a program which, when put into effect, brought immediate results in people's lives. This same program is still used today in all of the Mission Teens centers and the results are still phenomenal.

SUCCESS RATE

Since 1969, over 25,000 people have come into the various Mission Teens centers.   In our annual review, we hear from about 57% of our graduates and, of those, approximately 87% are doing well.   In addition, approximately 40% of the non-graduates we hear from are doing well.   Many have gone into Christian ministries and some have stayed on to work in our centers.

A DAY AT THE MISSION

We treat each person in our center as a member of the family.   Junior staff members and higher-ranking residents teach the "younger" residents.   Senior Staff and directors handle the major problems and decisions.   Each one is expected to do his or her part to make the "family" run as smoothly as possible.   There are 5 1/2 hours of Bible study per day, and the training amounts to approximately 1 year of Bible school.   There is a comprehensive study of the New Testament and a general study of the Old

Testament.   The daily schedule varies slightly at the centers, but fundamentally remains the same.

THE TRAINING PROGRAM

Our purpose is to provide hope to the hopeless.   It is our goal to direct the people to the Lord Jesus to find love and a purpose for their lives, and to make disciples of them as the Bible directs.   The discipleship-training program is divided up into four phases, each lasting 2-4 months.   As the person proves that he/she can handle the increasing responsibilities of each phase, their privileges will increase. It is a highly structured program with a rigid daily schedule. Everyone is expected to obey the house rules and follow the schedule.   Infractions of the rules or schedule are corrected with writing assignments, loss of privileges or extra work chores.   The first phase of the training is a 2-month induction period with very few privileges or responsibilities.   Each individual is simply expected to follow the rules and will begin to understand how to seek the Lord.

The next two phases add some general household responsibilities, which will add normal life pressures and cause the person to seek the Lord for help.   Privileges in these two phases include phone calls and visits from immediate family (and pastoral or legal counsel) only.   No friends are allowed to visit or call any person in the discipleship training.   In the final phase, the person is in "counselor training."   They will counsel one person each day and make a report to senior staff.   They are expected to be a good example in the house and to learn to help others as they were helped.

Upon completion of the program, the person may be offered an additional 10-12 month staff-training program.

FUNDING & EXPENSES

Mission Teens, Inc. is a not-for-profit 501 (C) 3 faith ministry. We do not charge for our services, and we do not receive any funding from the government. All of our support comes from concerned individuals and a few churches who are sensitive to the type of work we do. We do not receive any denominational funding (We are non-denominational). Each of our centers is expected to raise its own support from local sources. We do not charge anyone for the services we provide. Our goal is to help people who have life-controlling problems, such as drug or alcohol addictions, by ministering the Gospel of Jesus Christ to them. We believe that the Gospel should be free to all.

THE APPLICATION PROCESS

Adults (ages 18 and up) can apply to any of our centers for help. Admission is on a bed availability basis. Our centers are open to both men and women. All we ask is that the person is willing to seek God for the answer to all life's problems and be willing to follow the schedule of the program. Prospective residents should call the Overseer at the center of their choice. A preliminary interview will be done by phone or in person.

ONCE YOU'VE CALLED

We do require some initial blood tests (and a pregnancy test for women) before accepting a person. Also, the incoming resident may be required to have a return ticket (or the equivalent). It is important to know that the program is highly structured and if a person is incapable of adhering to program rules and guidelines they may not be permitted to stay. The return ticket is used in the event that we must ask a person to leave.

Any serious health or legal problems should be taken care of before coming into the center. Only emergency medical care will be sought for the person while in the training program, and any medical expenses are the responsibility of the resident. Typically, only non-addictive, non-narcotic medications will be permitted at any center.

OUR STAFF

Almost all of our staff are graduates of the discipleship training program.   They do not receive any salary, but work as missionaries, giving back their life to serve the Lord by reaching out to others.   The Assistant Executive Directors at each center work directly with the Executive Director to train the staff, oversee the general condition of the buildings and raise the necessary support, as well as teach, counsel, etc.   Each center also has an Overseer who is in charge of daily operations.   Anyone seeking admission into a center needs to call the Overseer at that center.

OUR MISSION STATEMENT

The purpose of a Mission Teens Inc. is to witness unto Jesus Christ in the world, in the power of the Holy Spirit, with a particular emphasis to young people, but not to the exclusion of anyone.

We know that Jesus Christ is the answer to everyone's needs. We will provide any and all facilities necessary to evangelize, educate and disciple any persons spiritually, physically, vocationally and psychologically as the Holy Spirit of God leads and directs.   We reserve the right to engage in any business we feel led to enter into in order to further the purpose of this Mission.

This organization is to be non-profit, supported by God, through people as He works individually in their hearts, primarily purposed in proclaiming Jesus Christ, to whom be all glory and honor.

This is to be His work; we are His servants.

Our individual purpose is to trust Him, to obey Him and to praise Him.   Truly He is worthy of all of our praise.

LOCATIONS

Administration
Mission Teens, Inc.
PO Box 131
Glendora, NJ 08029
(856) 782-7771

Northport, Alabama
Genesis MBTC
PO Box 869
Northport, AL 35476
(205) 267-0293

Tuscumbia, Alabama
Restoration Ranch
PO Box 767
Tuscumbia, AL 35647
(256) 381-0930

Marked Tree, Arkansas
God's New Life MBTC
PO Box 166
Marked Tree, AR 72365
(870) 358-4851

Paragould, Arkansas
Grace MBTC
PO Box 1035
Paragould, AR 72450
(870) 573-6414

Honey Dew, California
Mountain of Mercy
PO Box 55
Honey Dew, CA 95545
(707) 601-3403

Ft. Lauderdale, Florida
Sonrise MBTC
PO Box 5681
Ft. Lauderdale, FL 33310
(954) 485-0951

Savannah, Georgia
Savannah MBTC
1000 E Victory Drive
Savannah, GA 31405
(912) 234-7000

Jerseyville, Illinois
First Fruits MBTC
PO Box 176
Jerseyville, IL 62052
(618) 498-3560

Brazil, Indiana
House of Hope
PO Box 283
Brazil, IN 47834
(812) 446-1717

Cresco, Iowa
Midwest MBTC
PO Box 354
Cresco, IA 52136
(563) 547-3286

Greenville, Kentucky
Set Free MBTC
PO Box 554
Greenville, KY 42345
(270) 377-0075

Salyersville, Kentucky
Kentucky MBTC
PO Box 293
Salyersville, KY 41465
(606) 349-7607

Gaastra, Michigan
Mission Bible Training Center
PO Box 248
Gaastra, MI 49927
(906) 265-6247

Holcomb, Missouri
Freedom House
PO Box 221
Holcomb, MO 63852
(573) 371-2020

Norma, New Jersey
Mission Teens
PO Box 52
Norma, NJ 08347
(856) 691-9855

Hillsboro, Ohio
Ohio MBTC
PO Box 529
Hillsboro, OH 45133
(937) 509-0373

Portland, Oregon
Northwest MBTC
2724 N Ainsworth Street
Portland, OR 97217
(503) 289-7758

Crossville, Tennessee
Crossville MBTC
PO Box 452
Crossville, TN 38557
(931) 484-9935

DONATIONS:
Our program is free to any person who is willing to seek God for the answers to their problems.   But, operating this free program generates high expenses.   We cannot meet the needs of struggling people without the support of faithful partners in ministry such as you.

If you would like to make a donation to our organization you can do so via standard mail or securely online:
God's New Life MBTC
P.O.Box 166
Marked Tree, AR   72365
(870) 358-4851

Mission Teens, Inc. is a non-profit 501 (C) 3 organization. Donations made to our ministry are tax deductible.

WE   ARE   GRATEFUL   FOR   YOUR   SUPPORT.

Made in the USA
Lexington, KY
25 June 2017